THE GLOBALIST AGENDA IS REAL,

MAN-MADE AND DANGEROUS

The great friendship between

the Great Reset and the Covid-19

The globalist agenda is real, man-made and dangerous.
The great friendship between the Great Reset and Covid-19

Written by César Andrés Muñoz Madrigal between December 2020 and January 2021.

L'Hospitalet de Llobregat, Barcelona, Spain.

CONTENT

3

Foreword

On May 16th, 2013, then-US President Barack Obama said on his Twitter account: "Ninety-seven percent of scientists agree that climate change is real, man-made and dangerous." This is where the name of the title of this book comes from. President Barack Obama very possibly knew that what he was saying was false and not sufficiently proven, since presidents have always advisers or consultants who guide and inform them about different topics for decision making, but the truth is that the theory of climate change is part of the dogmas of a globalist agenda, and that the then president of the United States Barack Obama is simply a promoter and spokesman for that agenda like many other politicians around the world subject to it.

The funny thing about this statement is that there is not really a ninety-seven percent agreement among scientists that climate change is real, but that the percentage is much lower as I will explain later in the chapter on global warming, nor It has been proved that the dangerous climate change theory (because it is simply an unproven theory, even if they want to affirm it) or previously called global warming is man-made or really dangerous.

In fact, the theory of global warming, so widely and repeatedly disseminated by the media, was renamed "global warming" to "climate change" after many catastrophic predictions in this regard were not fulfilled (disappearance of glaciers, rise in sea level that would theoretically make beaches, islands or entire regions disappear by the past year 2020, extreme temperatures, etc.), in the same way that a political party is baptized with a different name when it has come out to the spotlight some case of great corruption within it, and they want to wash the image of it by changing its name.

So with many ideas in mind, I dedicate this book to all those people who are considering 2021 now or who will ask themselves in later years in what phase of history we are, where are we going to end up and what the world will be like after the present. pandemic (or plandemic = plan + pandemic = planned pandemic).

This book should also serve as a warning to sailors, may them be of christian faith or of any other belief, since although there are non-religious people who agree with some of the dogmas of the globalist agenda such as the LGTBIQ + ideology, or with abortion or euthanasia , possibly not so much with other dogmas of this agenda such as massive and uncontrolled migration between nations, or the fact that with the excuse that countries are going to cause global warming with the emission of greenhouse gases, the supranational leaders of the globalist agenda prevent a poor sovereign nation from creating its own industry or infrastructures, thus preventing its development, which is also due to this supranational agenda imposed in order to progressively empty the nation of its cultural identity, of its sovereignty political and financial and economic independence. It is also possible that many people do not agree, for example, with another of the dogmas of the globalist agenda such as the legalization of drug trafficking and consumption, which is used as a measure of social and economic subversion and openly promoted by the business tycoon George Soros.

Thus neither the existence of the globalist agenda nor its intentions against the interests of democratic states should be questioned, since David Rockefeller himself, billionaire banker and businessman of the Rockefeller dynasty, founder of globalist supranational organizations such as the Trilateral Commission, a member of the board of directors of the Council on Foreign Relations since 1949 and a participating member of the Bilderberg Club since its inauguration, etc. wrote in his book entitled "Memories" which was published in 2002: "Some accuse me of working against the United States and of being an internationalist having created a global economy and politics, not only do I plead guilty but I feel proud about it."

In fact, this statement by David Rockefeller implies two things: the recognition that the globalist agenda exists and that it works against the interests of sovereign nations, that is, it does not have very good intentions. Therefore when we speak of the globalist agenda, we should not think that it is a "conspiracy" theory any more, but something that its own members have recognized as true.

However, we must not confuse the globalist agenda, which is a supranational world agenda imposed on nations with globalization. In fact, globalization is the beautiful fact of being able to enjoy something that is manufactured in another country, for example, or of being able to connect globally via videoconference, that is, it is a global interconnection process allowed mainly by the internet and the new technologies enabling to interact with people from different parts of the globe or to be able to obtain products and services from other parts of the world.

On the other hand, there are many people who believe that after the pandemic is over and with time everything will return to normal, that is, we will consume, work, travel, etc. as before March 2020, while the leaders of supranational globalist entities such as the president of the World Economic Forum himself, many media, political leaders and bankers affirm that it will not be the case, and that after the Covid-19 pandemic is over, there will be a different "new normality" after a Great Reset, but not the same normality than before the pandemic.

In fact, the expression "new normality" has already emerged among leaders of supranational entities, politicians, health workers and economists around the world in a short time just after the Covid-19 pandemic was declared by the UN in early March 2020. And so curious is precisely that this expression was coined and adopted practically simultaneously by leaders around the world as if a power above them had imposed it. Generally, when a new reality occurs in a scenario where there is full freedom of action and expression, there would be people who would explain it with some words and other people with others, but precisely a series of terms such as "new normality" began to be used and resonated simultaneously in the media around the world.

Obviously I know that what was said in the previous paragraph sounds a bit like a paranoid conspiracy, but as the reader progresses through this short book, he/she will realize that it is not a conspiracy theory but a real agenda, man-made and dangerous, the globalist agenda, which many leaders, such as the last three Catholic popes including the current Pope Francis, have commonly referred to as a "New World Order", whose acronym in English would be "NWO" (New Word Arder), as it is often known.

1

Introduction and presentation of the general scenario

We live in a world marked by a globalist agenda and each time it is exposed in a more evident and open way. Despite this, on the one hand there are many people who do not really believe that this agenda exists, or who think that if there is one, it cannot really influence the governments of the nations of the world to change their policies or decisions. For this reason, this book has the mission among others to show the evidences of the existence of the globalist agenda, or at least some of them and the clearest evidence points to these people who doubt it, and that these supranational globalist entities really pressure governments to take concrete measures against the democratic interests of sovereign nations, and that they really represent a danger to people of any belief, since what is at stake is the survival of democracy, and of our individual rights and freedoms.

So what are the dogmas of the globalist agenda and what is the reason for imposing these dogmas?

The dogmas of the globalist agenda are basically:

1. The theory of global warming, now called climate change.
2. The LGTBIQ + ideology
3. Extreme feminism
4. The abortion
5. Euthanasia
6. Mass and uncontrolled immigration
7. The legalization of drugs

Basically these are the dogmas of the globalist agenda because they justify as massive and uncontrolled immigration that there is a supranational government that controls the countries and their borders, and they make it easier for these nations to gradually lose their national cultural identity, as for example with the massive arrival of immigrants, which little by little would allow these nations to be emptied of their values and sovereignty.

On the other hand, the theory of global warming, which allows, for example, controlling that certain countries do not develop economically with the excuse that they are going to cause global warming with their gas emissions. In addition, the discourse of the fight against dangerous climate change through the transformation of companies into environmentally responsible green companies, or through the implementation of environmental projects of all kinds, is an efficient way to capture part of the public budgets of nations or to capture private funds that are then often used by governments to grant favors to some privileged groups that in turn will give their vote to these politicians. In other words, the climate change excuse is perfect for raising money or imposing taxes that can then be used under the table for other purposes. Moreover with the global warming excuse governments have a reason to restrict natality which is one of the goals of the globalist agenda, as the more people on the world, the more CO_2 is emitted into the atmosphere upon expiration and more potential to emit greenhouse gases there will be.

On the other hand, both the LGTBIQ + agenda, abortion and euthanasia allow to help reduce the world population, since according to the globalist agenda, planet Earth is overpopulated and it is necessary to reduce its population because resources do not grow as quickly than population but much more slowly, that is, it is based on a Malthusian conception of population, as the 18th century British scholar and Anglican clergyman Thomas Robert Malthus put it this way: "When no obstacle prevents it, the population is doubling every 25 years, growing from period to period, in a geometric progression. The means of subsistence, in the most favorable circumstances, are only increased in an arithmetic progression. " Also later this same idea of population growth versus the growth of the means of subsistence was also adopted by the Club of Rome in 1968, a non-governmental organization that is the precedent of the European Union. Thus, the dogmas of the globalist agenda such as the defense of the LGTBQ + ideology, abortion, euthanasia, etc. although they are defended by supranational globalist agents as human rights that must be granted to people, in reality they are only means to achieve their globalist goals. In other words, the elites who impose the globalist agenda do not really care about the rights of gay, lesbian, trans people, etc., or don't really care about pregnant women when they promote abortion or sick and elderly people with the euthanasia, since these are millionaire elites from the world of finance, technology, pharmaceutical companies, etc. who have no need to defend these rights, but simply they do it and promote them in order to achieve the objectives of the globalist agenda:

Regarding the legalization of the trade and use of drugs, what the globalist agenda seeks with this dogma is the increase in health problems, the dismemberment of families whose individuals destroy their lives using drugs and of the society affected by the mafia of the drugs, due to organized crime related to drug trafficking and the creation of an economy that lives off drug trafficking, which would cause political and social tensions such as those caused by the Latin American drug cartels. Ultimately, the objective of drug legalization is to subvert the order of society to justify the intervention of a supranational globalist government, which would also control the borders at will.

Obviously the statement that the dogmas of the globalist agenda are not for the good of the people but to achieve the objective of population reduction among others, is very shocking and many readers will find it implausible, but throughout the book we will prove its veracity, since in fact the globalist agenda is not a friend of real democracy, but of a new world government that in an authoritarian way controls more and more the politics and economy of the different nations, that would become mere protectorates devoid of real political and economic authority.

It is also logical that people are suspicious that these dogmas hide a global agenda with malevolent intentions, as these dogmas have been constantly and intensely advertised and promoted by media monopolies in recent decades, so they have become accepted truths as if they were really proven, that is, they have become almost religions (the religion of climate change or global warming, the religion of the LGTBIQ + ideology, the religion of abortion, etc.). Thus, the strategy for the success in the implementation of these dogmas also consists precisely in that their constant repetition to the people through the media over time makes them be believed as proven truths, which are simply accepted by people without further questioning.

2

Personal testimony

In fact, in 2019 I used to watch YouTube videos of economists, traders and experts in the field regarding the global evolution of the economy in the coming years, and in fact in that year many videos could already be found on YouTube by experts who said that for the year 2020 or 2021 a huge end-of-cycle crisis was expected, which would be much greater than the last global crisis of 2008 that began in 2007 in the United States with the subprime mortgage crisis or junk mortgages. When they said that it would be an end-of-cycle crisis much bigger than that of 2008, I was surprised since this crisis was really big, and even countries like Spain had not yet finished recovering from it in 2019.

Basically the experts in these YouTube videos explained that in 2019 a global slowdown of the economy was already taking place despite the fact that the stock markets of some countries, especially the US stock markets, were at all-time highs. These experts added that the slowdown was mainly caused by the Brexit in the United Kingdom and the trade war between the United States and China, which obviously had an influence on the world economy, these two nations being the first two largest economies on the planet. In addition, in many videos it was anticipated that this super-crisis at the end of the capitalist cycle would be accompanied by what they already called a Great Reset or a Great Restart worldwide. In other words, the Great Reset that the International Economic Forum would propose in 2020 had already been announced at the beginning of 2019, and it would mean the end of capitalism as we know it today.

Thus I wondered what devastating event or events would produce this great end-of-cycle crisis, because the trade war between the United States and China with the American stock markets at all-time highs, plus the effects of Brexit, along with some other macroeconomic factors, did not seem to me to be sufficient reasons to cause an economic debacle of this size. And so the year 2020 finally arrived and the Covid-19 pandemic as we all know, or plan-demic as many people call it, who claim that it is a plan to use the pandemic to induce collective fear, control the population through confinements and restrictions of rights and freedoms, stop national economies to provoke a global economic crisis of gigantic scale, and thus advance the globalist agenda and justify a great economic, political and social reset.

This great reset, for example, was already announced on December 31, 2019 as something totally necessary for the year 2020 in a video on YouTube by the world's leading financial and business publication "Financial Times". This short video by the Financial Times is still on YouTube (link to the video in the bibliography at the end of this book), and basically comes to say that an economic and financial reset is necessary because it is increasingly important for the younger generations to have investors, companies and entrepreneurs that when investing or running their businesses do so thinking about caring for the environment, avoiding global warming, avoiding eating animal meat replacing it for a vegetarian diet to precisely avoid dangerous climate change, etc.

Is such a drastic measure like an economic, financial, political and social reset really necessary just because of wanting to create a more respectful world with the environment, being in fact something that has already been taken into account, that has already been legislated about and applied in many companies for decades?. In a few words: green and environmental respectful policies are nothing new to justify a world Great Reset.

On the other hand, for more than two years I had suspected that the so repeated by the official media as the theory of man-made global warming, or now called "climate change" was false, a name change that has occurred as the catastrophic predictions for the climate that many scientists had done in the last decades of the twentieth century did not occur, such as that in 2020 there would no longer be glaciers or beaches because they would have disappeared due to the rise in sea level caused by the melting of glaciers, melting which in turn is produced by the increase in global terrestrial temperature in theory.

My suspicions that the man-made global warming theory was false were due to the fact that in mid-2017 I lost all my savings doing trading (speculation with financial assets), and at the end of this very same year I wrote my first book "The dark side of trading and of financial markets , denouncing the deceptions of trading courses, fundamental and technical analysis, and through the process of doing trading and losing all my savings, I developed a skeptical side to any supposed truth or theory proclaimed massively and repeatedly by the mass media, such as the case of the theory of anthropogenic global warming, which means that the global warming is caused by humans, theories that as the times goes by become widely accepted truths by the population who do not even ponder their veracity.

But I also started to watch more videos regarding the theory of global warming and I realized that there were a lot of scientists from fields related to climate science, such as geology or physics who did not agree with the theory of global warming, and that they had also written scientific publications about it. In addition, many of these scientists who don't support the theory of global warming in many cases were scientists with extensive experience in the study of climate, and with a much more complete and even more related resume to the climate sciences than many other scientists who were in favor of the man-made global warming theory.

I also saw other videos on YouTube against the opinion of dangerous global warming or the supposed consensus of 97% of scientists on this very fact, for example from Dr. Don Easterbrook, emeritus professor of geology at the Western Washington University, with more than 50 years of experience and knowledge in climate change, he is one of many high-ranking scientists who express his opposition to the theory of global warming, as he himself explained in a session in the US Senate dated from March 26, 2013, specifically in the Senate Committee on Energy, Environment and Telecommunications, or for example Willie Wei-Hock Soon, who isa Malaysian astrophysicist and aerospace engineer employed as a part-time researcher in the Division of Solar and Stellar Physics (SSP) of the Harvard-Smithsonian Center for Astrophysics, who was awarded the Petr Beckmann Prize in 2004.

Also in my research I discovered that against the IPCC (Intergovernmental Panel on Climate Change) which depends on the UN (United Nations), another scientific panel called the Non-Governmental Panel on Climate Change (NIPCC, for its acronym in English) had been created and had published abundant scientific publications explaining why man-made global warming is not scientifically well proven or real, saying for example among many other scientific reasons, that there have been other times in history warmer than today in which there were fewer or no cars, fewer or no factories that produced greenhouse gases, such as the 1st century BC, the Middle Ages or the 1930s.

Viewing these videos on YouTube and reading scientific publications from the Non-Governmental Panel on Climate Change led me to find out about the lies of the global warming theory, lies that are mainly used to prevent certain nations from prospering by raising their own industry or economy with the excuse by supranational globalist entities that if they do so they will cause more global warming. Thus these nations, as well as those on the African continent or in Latin America, are condemned to permanent poverty, although to a large extent they survive thanks to the aid of the World Bank, or the International Monetary Fund, which are globalist entities.

Also in a discussion on WhatsApp with a friend, he told me that water vapor actually affects the greenhouse effect, but the fact that there is water vapor in the atmosphere is the consequence of heating on the surface and not the other way around. So I was trying to argue that water vapor is the main greenhouse gas in the atmosphere and not carbon dioxide, due to the transmission of heat by convection from water, in which the hottest water vapor particles in the lower part of the atmosphere rise and the cooler water vapor particles descend near the surface (according to the NIPCC report of September 2017 titled: "Surprises of Global Warming" written by the scientist who died last year Siegfried Fred Singer). In fact through Dr. Willie Soon I confirmed that the sun is the main agent of global warming, and although we think we know a lot about it and that pretty much only its distance to a region of the earth determines whether it is more or less hot, the sun also has solar cycles of about eleven years of duration in which sunspots of different types and sizes appear and disappear that indicate the sun's level of activity. There is also clear evidence of a strong urban island heat effect that pollutes the temperature data sets collected by governments, according to this same astrophysicist and climate scientist, Dr. Soon, as he explained, when he gave the presentation entitled "The sun also warms" in the 16th Annual Friends of Science Event, April 10, 2019 at the Red & White Club in Calgary, Alberta (Canada). This same scientist said in this same conference that there are many types of sunspots that appear and disappear over time that are of different sizes and shapes that influence the energy radiated by the sun in different ways, but that this solar irradiance varies even more than sunspots.

I myself have come to the conclusion that carbon dioxide has been demonized, because after all, all human beings and most animals breathe oxygen and give off carbon dioxide, so the more people in the world and the more livestock and animals there are, the more carbon dioxide there will be in the atmosphere, the more greenhouse effect there will be and the higher ground temperatures in theory there will be. So, should we stop multiplying ourselves and raising animals and livestock to avoid global warming of the atmosphere? It seems like a silly question, but the truth is that it makes you think. In addition, plants need sunlight and carbon dioxide to grow, so the more carbon dioxide in the atmosphere, the more vegetation and plants will grow as it is understandable.

In fact, it has been observed that in 2015 there was more vegetation and green areas covering an area of 36 million km_2 on planet Earth, approximately twice the area of the United States, than in 1982 due to the fertilization of regions with CO_2, and tree planting programs in China and intensive agriculture programs in both India and China.

Finally, we could ask ourselves: was God wrong when He created beings that breathe oxygen and expel carbon dioxide, causing involuntarily a dangerous greenhouse effect in the atmosphere for the climate and for life on Earth?

What is the globalist agenda?

The globalist agenda is an agenda promoted by supranational organizations and entities formed by financial, technological, pharmaceutical or telecommunications industry magnates with the intention of controlling the world and nation states both politically and economically.

It starts mainly from a Malthusian vision of the population growth as we have already said, which was adopted as a precedent by the Club of Rome, an international non-governmental organization founded in 1968. The Malthusian vision of the population growth considers that it is multiplying much faster than resources and therefore it is necessary to reduce or at least control population growth through its dogmas: climate change, LGTBIQ + ideology and policies, abortion, euthanasia, massive and uncontrolled immigration, legalization of drugs.

Thus, climate change is the umbrella doctrine of the globalist agenda to justify the impediment to the economic growth and development of nations, and it is the the perfect excuse to monopolize public budgets and private funds for their objectives.

To control demographic growth, LGTBIQ + policies are also used, since homosexual people cannot have children among themselves, although they can adopt them more and more regularly, and also break with the social structure of the traditional family, which of course is the one that has always in history being in charge of bringing children to the world producing population growth. The traditional family is formed by a father, a mother and children, which is the basic social structure in christianity, and which throughout history has been a pillar in the development of Western societies, whose values the globalist agenda tries to make disappear. They also clearly use abortion and euthanasia to more directly limit population growth, both against the prolife christian values.

Also in order to progressively erode or eradicate the national identity and cultural values of each nation, lax migration policy is used between the borders of the countries. Thus, with an almost majority immigrant population in sovereign nations, the citizens of these countries are more moldable to globalist dogmas since their national identity is partially eroded and dissolved, and chaos at the borders becomes the perfect excuse so that supranational entities may replace the nation-states in their internal policies and in the control of their borders

However, as It has already been said of all the dogmas of the globalist agenda, the umbrella dogma or doctrine at the present time is climate change or global warming, because it allows justifying a political, economic and social reset with the argument that the economic and productive system prior to the Covid-19 pandemic has failed, since supposedly under that capitalist system human beings have been destroying and polluting the environment, emitting excess greenhouse gases that cause an increase in atmospheric and terrestrial temperatures, despite the fact that even the president of the World Economic Forum, Klaus Schwab, acknowledges that in the late 20th and early 21st centuries, poverty, illiteracy and infant death have been drastically reduced, and new classes have emerged with the capacity to, as for example in China, that is, we have recently lived in the last decades in a much better world than in past times. Despite this, and without the express consent of the world population, supranational entities such as the World Economic Forum want to impose their globalist agenda, an agenda imposed by an elite who have not been democratically elected by the people.

Therefore, the imposition of this globalist agenda is basically a dictatorship imposed by an elitist oligarchy made up of millionaires from various economic areas such as finance, large technology companies so called "Big Tech", large pharmaceutical companies or so called "Big Pharma", major media groups and politicians of different countries.

Main visible icons of the globalist agenda

George soros

Although one of the reasons why the imposition and extension of the globalist agenda has been successful is the fact that the globalist agenda has been kept secret for decades, precisely in recent years one of the top icons of this agenda, Györgi Schwartz, better known as George Soros, born in 1930 in Hungary, who as a young man already collaborated with the Nazi occupiers in his country for the deportation of Jews to the Auschwitz concentration camps, of which he has confessed not to regret or have the least remorse about it. In short, Soros is a Hungarian business and finance magnate, speculator, philanthropist, and sponsor of subversive political movements that can undermine the power of nation states to empty states of their authority or transform them into simple protectorates of supranational globalist entities. He is particularly known as the man who broke the Bank of England in October 1992, with a speculative operation of his Hedge Fund or investment fund.

Thus by some estimates, by 2017 Soros had spent more than twelve trillion dollars ($3 million millions) to fund political causes in accordance with the goals of the globalist agenda. In fact, the power of Soros, however, has extended beyond simply financing the globalist agenda on an international scale, also promoting political programs in presidents of government, launching legislative changes in different nations and counting on an extraordinary influence in international organizations that have the objectives of implementing the globalist agenda.

Thus, thanks to the billions of dollars spent by Soros, the dogmas of the globalist agenda that we will see next, such as illegal and mass immigration, gender ideology, drug legalization, global warming theory, abortion, euthanasia, etc. They have been promoted in all parts of the world except in those countries where there have been politicians who resist the imposition of this agenda, such as until now in the United States by President Donald Trump, in Russia by President Putin, in China by President Xi Jinping, in Brazil with President Jair Bolsonaro, in Hungary with President Viktor Orbán, etc. Yes, the majority of them are presidents of the political right and not very popular, such as Trump, Orbán or Bolsonaro, who by the way share the same faith: protestantism.

George Soros has also been an advisor to governments such as the current president of Spain himself, Pedro Sánchez, of the Spanish Socialist Workers' Party (PSOE), and thus met with Sánchez in June 2018, after the triumph of the motion of censure in the Spanish Parliament that ended with the resignation of then President Mariano Rajoy due to corruption. By then it was well known that George Soros had been financing the failed independence process in Catalonia, obviously not because Soros felt Catalan, but because the tensions created by these Catalan independence movements created great national political instability in Spain, and therefore they were favorable for the implantation of the globalist agenda in this nation. In other words, the internal political tensions of nations undermine and erode their cultural identity, especially those that have to do with independence movements, and generate the perfect excuse for the imposition of a supranational globalist government that in theory would ensure the control of these tensions. On the other hand, at other times George Soros has not delivered directives in private to politicians, but has published in different media what national governments are supposed to do. Thus, in 2018, through the Spanish digital newspaper "el Confidencial", Soros said that about the Italian government coalition that was formed, the European Union could not try to teach Italy a lesson, because in that case the Italian electorate would re-elect the coalition of the 5-star movement (left-wing party) with the League (right-wing party), and so Soros attacked the immigration policy of the Italian government contrary to the uncontrolled entry of immigrants and in favor of border control.

Is it normal for a millionaire to tell sovereign nations what they should or should not do? In a democratic nation whose rulers have been partly elected by the people, no billionaire philanthropist should say what that government should or should not do, since it has no legitimacy or democratic backing to do it.

In fact, even George Soros 'influence in governments and international organizations is so real that Soros' entities themselves take pride in it. In this way in 2017 the Open Society Policy Institute and the Open Society network, both organizations dependent on George Soros, published the list of trusted allies of George Soros in the European Parliament, which included nothing more and nothing less than 226 deputies out of a total of 751, that is to say almost a third of the European Parliament with politicians from both the right and the political left.

Thus, the fact that almost a third of the European Parliament can be trusted by Soros's objectives, and that they are politicians from both the right and the political left, makes us think about the representativeness of this parliament, about the reasons why parliamentary candidates present themselves as candidates, and that few parties really defend the rights of citizens against the globalist agenda.

In addition, Soros, as American writer David Horowitz and American actor Richard Poe have extensively documented, has taken a multitude of steps to control USA politics, specifically taking over Democratic party politics. An example of this was the women's march that took place in Washington after Donald Trump took office as President of the United States on January 20, 2016. Thus, Soros subsidizes or maintains relations with at least 56 organizations that sponsored the march, such as the abortionist organization "Planned Parenthood".

Finally, we can also add that Soros has also influenced figures in favor of the globalist agenda, such as Pope Francis, as indicated in the book leaked by WikiLeaks regarding the May 2015 meeting of the North American directory of the Open Society Foundations (Soros' Foundations), where it is explained the delivery of $ 650,000 to finance the Pope's visit to the United States. Thus George Soros according to this book has counted on: "engaging the pope in matters of economic and social justice", which adds the Vatican to his globalist agenda.

Pope Francis and the Vatican

In a very significant way according to the majority of theologians of the bible, the great Babylon, mother of harlots or prostitutes, who is going to be judged in the bible book of Revelation in chapter 17 is the Vatican or the Catholic Church. Thus says the 17th chapter of Revelation from verses 1 to 9: "**17** One of the seven angels who had the seven bowls came and said to me, "Come, I will show you the punishment of the great prostitute, who sits by many waters. [2] With her the kings of the earth committed adultery, and the inhabitants of the earth were intoxicated with the wine of her adulteries."

[3] Then the angel carried me away in the Spirit into a wilderness. There I saw a woman sitting on a scarlet beast that was covered with blasphemous names and had seven heads and ten horns. [4] The woman was dressed in purple and scarlet, and was glittering with gold, precious stones and pearls. She held a golden cup in her hand, filled with abominable things and the filth of her adulteries. [5] The name written on her forehead was a mystery:

BABYLON THE GREAT

THE MOTHER OF PROSTITUTES

AND OF THE ABOMINATIONS OF THE EARTH.

[6] I saw that the woman was drunk with the blood of God's holy people, the blood of those who bore testimony to Jesus.

When I saw her, I was greatly astonished. [7] Then the angel said to me: "Why are you astonished? I will explain to you the mystery of the woman and of the beast she rides, which has the seven heads and ten horns. [8] The beast, which you saw, once was, now is not, and yet will come up out of the Abyss and go to its destruction. The inhabitants of the earth whose names have not been written in the book of life from the creation of the world will be astonished when they see the beast, because it once was, now is not, and yet will come.

[9] "This calls for a mind with wisdom. The seven heads are seven hills on which the woman sits."

In fact, the city of Rome, where the Vatican State is right next to it, is located on seven mountains, which have appeared many times in written popular culture. The seven hills of Rome are a series of headlands that have historically formed the heart of this city. So the seven hills of ancient Rome are according to Wikipedia:

- HeAventine(Collis Aventinus), (47 meters high).
- HeCapitoline(Capitolinus, which had two ridges: the Arx and the Capitolium), (50 meters high).
- HeCelio(Caelius, whose eastern extension was called Caeliolus), (50 meters high).
- HeEsquiline(Esquilinus, which had three peaks: the Cispius, the Fagutalis and theOpius), (64 meters high).
- HePalatine Hill(Collis Palatinus, whose three peaks were: the Cermalus or Germalus, the Palatium and the Velia), (51 meters high).
- HeQuirinal(Quirinalis, which had three peaks: the Latiaris, the Mucialis or Sanqualis, and the Salutaris), (61 meters high).
- HeViminal(Viminalis), (60 meters high).

Revelation 17:2 says: "With her the kings of the earth committed adultery, and the inhabitants of the earth became drunk with the wine of their immorality. In fact, both the Vatican and the Catholic Church have historically been characterized by supporting kings or politicians who more favored their economic or political interests, and not by supporting monarchs or politicians more in accordance with the religious and moral doctrines of the Catholic Church. .

We also see that the prostitute woman is dressed in purple and scarlet, and adorned with gold, precious stones and pearls that reminds us of the way popes are dressed and the sumptuousness and wealth found within Catholic temples.

And furthermore this prostitute according to verse 6 has gotten drunk with the blood of the saints and the martyrs of Jesus. Thus, for example, it is well known that in the Middle Ages the institution of the Catholic Church known as the Spanish Inquisition, founded by the Spanish Catholic kings in 1478 and which lasted almost four centuries until its abolition in 1834, condemned, burned and killed multitudes of Protestant christians for considering them heretics or witches.

In addition to this day, news continues to leak from the opaque businesses of the Vatican that have sometimes been used for money laundering, without forgetting the killings in the history of innocent people carried out in the name of God by the Catholic Church, or of the acts of pedophilia perpetrated by Catholic priests or bishops.

But since Pope John XXIII in the twentieth century, through John Paul II and Benedict XVI, all the popes of the twentieth century and of the beginning of the twenty-first century, have written or defended the need for a new world order in their encyclicals (letters addressed to the Catholic faithful on matters of faith or customs), speeches or interviews.

Thus, on January 1, 2004, one of the most relevant diplomatic initiatives of the papacy of John Paul II took place, launching the idea of a new world order precisely. Thus, Pope John Paul II affirmed that "more than ever, we need a new world order that makes use of the experience and the results achieved in these years by the United Nations."

The importance of this declaration stems from the fact that the Vatican state has the status of observer at the United Nations and diplomatic representation in more than 170 countries. Thus, its ability to act as a lobby for certain interests is quite large.

In fact, his successor Benedict XVI also in his encyclical "Caritas in Veritate" (Love in truth), signed on June 29, 2009 referred to the same need for a supranational government as follows: "To manage the world economy, to revive the economy hit by the crisis, to avoid any deterioration of the current crisis and the major imbalances that would result from it, to provide comprehensive and timely disarmament, food security and peace, to guarantee the protection of the environment and regulate migration: for all this, there is an urgent need for a true world political authority ".

Thus, as we can see in this paragraph of the encyclical "Caritas in Veritate", the dogmas and objectives of the globalist agenda that we will see below appear quite clearly, such as the protection of the environment against climate change, migration and of course the need for a world supranational government.

According to this same encyclical, this world political authority should regulate financial markets and put an end to inequalities and distortions of the capitalist development, which as we will see, is one of the Great Reset dogmas advocated by the World Economic Forum, referring to which we can read in its website, that is, the transition to a world socialist system, in which there is more economic and social equality, but where people are also poorer.

So also in this encyclical Pope Benedict XVI affirmed that the creation of this new world order would be based on emptying national governments of their powers. In textual words of the encyclical: "this transformation will be made at the cost of a gradual and balanced transfer of a part of the powers of each nation to a world authority and regional authorities."

Later, Pope Francis, who had praised Fidel Castro's dictatorship in Cuba, in his prologue to the book "Dialogues between John Paul II and Fidel Castro", which was published in 1998 when he was Archbishop of Buenos Aires, established connections and parallels between the dogmas of the Catholic Church and the theoretical bases of the dictatorship of Fidel Castro in Cuba, and in turn relating it to the theoretical bases of Karl Marx's socialism. Thus, on May 24, 2014, Pope Francis published the encyclical letter "Laudato si" (Praised) which states the following: "Climate change is real and dangerous. A new system of world governance is needed to deal with this unprecedented threat. This new political authority would be in charge of pollution and development of poor countries and regions."

And so many more things could be told, arguing why Pope Francis supports the globalist agenda and is one of its main icons, but we could highlight his recent open support for LGTBIQ + unions. Thus, in October 2020, Pope Francis expressed for the first time his support for the legalization of civil unions for same-sex couples, through an interview for a documentary that premiered at the Rome Film Festival.

Thus Pope Francis said in the film titled "Francesco": "Gay people have the right to be in a family. They are children of God and they have the right to a family. No one should be expelled or feel miserable about it."

Bill Gates

We all know Bill Gates for being the billionaire founder of the computer company Microsoft, whose operating systems almost everyone has used. But currently he is also known for creating the Bill and Melinda Gates foundation that, together with campaigns and projects to eliminate poverty, increase hygiene measures and help poor countries, promote global vaccination worldwide for different diseases, and for being the largest financier of the World Health Organization, which, as a member of the UN and as a good supranational entity, tries to impose the dogmas of the globalist agenda on the nations, that is, abortion, euthanasia, etc., although for example abortion may not be the most convenient measure for the reproductive, physical and mental health of the mother.

What is not so well known about Bill Gates is that he is in favor of reducing the world's population, and that just after Microsoft was denounced for abusing its monopoly power by the United States Department of Justice in early May 1998, referring to the Windows operating system business and the sale of computers, It is when Bill Gates created the Bill and Melinda Gates Foundation, with the first objective of promoting and facilitating abortion, like his very own father, who was a board member from the abortion organization Planned Parenthood, did. Thus, Bill Gates became a philanthropist, that is to say, one more billionaire who takes care of the "good" of humanity following his own agenda, through his foundations and organizations, as many other billionaires like George Soros do.

It is also not widely known that between approximately 2,000 and 2017 the Bill and Melinda Gates Foundation tested the polio vaccine on children in India, of which some 496,000 children were left paralyzed, and after several legal actions in India they managed to expel the Bill Foundation and Melinda Gates from that nation.

In addition, Bill Gates as a good billionaire philanthropist belongs to the World Economic Forum that meets in Davos, Switzerland in January every year (although in 2021 they will meet in the month of May in Singapore). In this way, there is no doubt that Bill Gates is one of the magnates, who of course organizes the globalist agenda like any of the other participants in the International Economic Forum. Thus, precisely this organization is the one that promotes the world Great Reset including all the dogmas of the globalist agenda.

Bill Gates also supports and is part of the ambitious ID2020 project, which is an example of what new technologies, such as 5G technology or the Internet of Things, can help to achieve control of society and the migration of a capitalist system in the Western world towards a socialist one, as the International Economic Forum claims with the Great Reset. Thus, this project proposes the global digitization with biometric data and blockchain technology of all people, and has become another of the controversial undertakings of the computer magnate, in this case associated with the historic Rockefeller financial dynasty. ID2020 ("Digital Identity 2020") was founded between 2017 and 2018 by The Rockefeller Foundation, Microsoft and Gavi or the "Vaccine Alliance". The latter entity associates both the Bill and Melinda Gates Foundation and the world's leading laboratories. Together with these founding partners are associated the Hyperledger corporations, dedicated to blockchain technology; IRespond and Simprints, organizations dedicated to the use of biometric data for digital identity; the ICC, the United Nations International Computing Center, among others.

What is the goal of ID2020?. To identify each person above the identity records of each national state. According to the developers themselves, in the future, this digital identity will be necessary to access education, health, social benefits, political rights such as voting and carrying out economic transactions. It is effectively a globalist project in which people would have a kind of digital tattoo with electronic ink with all their data, but which basically aims to control the population using new technologies, and which roots with the concept of transhumanism, that is, the implantation of technological and digital devices in the human body and brain to theoretically improve the human species and produce a supposed evolution, turning the "evolved" human beings into demigods.

Thus, the fact of getting a digital tattoo that would have all our information printed in, reminds us of what in the bible book of Revelation is known as the mark of the beast "666", which is placed on the forehead or hand, and without which people will not be able to buy or sell.

Although in fact similar technologies have already begun to be used in China in 2020, and thus under the constant gaze of thousands of street cameras, Chinese citizens are already beginning to be evaluated according to their behavior through a controversial «system of social credit », in which the score is key when obtaining a loan or being able to travel for example. Thus it is impossible not to find similarities between the reality that exists in China and the omnipresent and vigilant "Big Brother" of George Orwell in "1984", or the science fiction that is portrayed on Netflix with the series "Black Mirror".

The international organizations of the globalist agenda

These are the organizations, entities, commissions or non-governmental forums of an international character as widely known as the United Nations, the International Monetary Fund, the World Health Organization, the World Economic Forum, etc. that are not born out of democratic mechanisms nor are they born out of the popular will.

Or the ones fairly known as the Bilderberg Club, the Council on Foreign Relations or the one barely known as the Trilateral Commission.

The well-known banker and businessman David Rockefeller, a great promoter of the globalist agenda in the 20th century, mentioned among other globalist international organizations in his memories book published in 2002 the following ones:

The Council on Foreign Relations, which was founded in 1921, with the intention of supporting the League of Nations, the direct antecedent of the UN, and which theoretically sought to inform American citizens about world reality. Thus, It supported the intervention of the United States in World War II, and in the decade of the fifties of the twentieth century he defended the control of population growth with reproductive containment, that is, he supported that couples did not have many children. David Rockefeller himself served on the board of directors since 1949 along with financiers and lawyers, and in the 1980s the Council on Foreign Relations already covered environmental, economic development and all kinds of causes.

The Bilderberg Club, whose first meeting took place in May 1955, is named after the hotel where the first meeting was held, which was attended by fifty people from eleven Western nations, including David Rockefeller.

The Trilateral Commission, founded in the early 1970s, it sought to extend global dominance beyond what the United States could do. It was also created by David Rockefeller and Zbigniew Brzezinski, and held its first meeting in Tokyo in October 1973, bringing together tycoons from Western Europe and Japan. It should be noted that in April 1984 all of its members were received by President Ronald Reagan in the White House, and whose work in the United States foreign policy has been more decisive in recent decades than that of the US Congress or Senate, especially thanks to politicians like Brzezinski.

The great global investment funds

We are referring specifically to Black Rock, the Vanguard group and State Street, so called "the Big Three".

So according to Wikipedia BlackRock is an American investment management company whose headquarters are in New York. It is considered the largest in the world in asset management, with assets under management valued at more than 5.1 trillion dollars ($5.1 million of millions) in 2016 according to the company, and it is a shareholder of the main pharmaceutical companies that have developed in 2020 the Covid-19 virus vaccines such as Pfizer or Moderna. Just by looking at its website one can see that it is a sponsor and promoter of the dogmas of the global agenda.

According to Wikipedia, The Vanguard Group is the largest investment fund manager in the world and the second largest provider of ETFs after iShares, a Blackrock company. It is also one of the main shareholders of pharmaceutical companies that have developed vaccines for the Covid-19 virus in 2020, such as Pfizer, Moderna or AstraZeneca.

State Street Corporation is according to Wikipedia an American finance services company and bank holding company based in Boston with operations around the world. It is the second bank in the United States on the list of oldest banks in continuous operation; its predecessor, Union Bank, was founded in 1792. State Street is ranked 15th on the list of the largest banks in the United States by assets. It is one of the largest asset management companies in the world, with $ 2.78 trillion under management and $ 33.12 trillion in custody and administration. It is the largest custodian bank in the world and one of the main shareholders of pharmaceutical companies like Pfizer and Moderna.

The big pharmaceutical companies or "Big Pharma"

Large pharmaceutical companies are also the great drivers of the globalist agenda, and there are often senior members of these companies in supranational globalist entities. In fact, it has been rumored that large pharmaceutical companies created the Covid-19 virus to recover from the economic losses caused by the health legislative reform brought by the Obama Care, approved in 2012 and that expanded health coverage in the United States for more people and circumstances, especially for people over 65 and for people with lower incomes.

The largest pharmaceutical companies according to their annual revenues are: Pfizer, Roche, Novarais, Merck, GlaxoSmithKline, Johnson & Johnson, AbbVie, Sanofi, Bristol Myers Squibb and AstraZeneca, as of March 4, 2020.

The big technological companies or "Big Tech"

We all know more or less the largest global technological companies, which according to their global revenues are in this order according to Fortune magazine's 2020 list (in American billions or thousand millions of US dollars), and published on Wikipedia (Amazon has been added to the list of retail and non-technology companies, with annual revenues of $ 280.522 billion, or 280,522 million US dollars).

1. Apple Annual revenue: $ 260.174 billion annually

2. Samsung Electronics $ 197.705 billion

3. Foxconn $ 178.869 billion

4. Alphabet (Google) $ 161.857 billion

5. Microsoft $ 125.843

6. Huawei $ 124.316

7. Dell Technologies $ 92.154

8. Hitachi $ 80.639

9. IBM $ 77.147

10. Sony $ 75.972

11.Intel $ 71.965

12. Facebook $ 70.697

13. Panasonic$ 68.897

14. HP Inc. $ 58.756

15.Tencent $ 54.613

16. LG Electronics $ 53.464

17. Cisco $ 51.904

18. Lenovo $ 50.716

Basically the strategy consists of the government legislating in favor of large technological companies so that they have privileges, including favorable fiscal and tax legislation, so these companies become an ally of the pro-globalist government of the day with the publication and promotion of the dogmas of the globalist agenda or the censorship of content of dissenting opinions against the official version of the government or censorship against patriotic (that defends the interests of sovereign nations against globalist interests) ideas, recently including censorship to the former president of the United States till January 19th 2020, Donald Trump. So this happened with the elimination of Donald Trump's Twitter account, or the suspension of his Facebook and Instagram accounts after the assault on the capitol in Washington DC on January 6th, 2021, based on an alleged instigation to violence and to political mutiny allegedly done by Trump, or for example the case of big social media websites like YouTube, Twitter, etc. since the beginning of the pandemic, blocking videos and suspending accounts of many YouTubers or twitter users, who spoke out against vaccines, fraud in the United States elections of November 3, 2020, or express dissenting opinions to the official ones of the governments regarding the pandemic.

The oligopoly of the big media conglomerates

Thus, the large media groups mainly Comcast, The Walt Disney Company, AT&T and ViacomCBS, followed by smaller groups such as Bertelsmann, Sony Corporation, News Corp, Fox Corporation, Hearst Communications, MGM Holding Inc., the Globo group and the Lagardère group. In other words, a dozen companies have 80% of the world's media production, which has turned the information market into a set of oligopolies that put the veracity and neutrality of the media at risk. That is why through these large groups it has been easy to spread the dogmas of the globalist agenda in an effective way and in a way almost unquestioned by the population.

Fortunately, more and more the population is getting informed through alternative media such as internet websites, blogs or private websites, private YouTubers, private Telegram channels, etc., whilst the pieces of news and information provided by the official media, including the written press, are more and more often questioned regarding its veracity specially during this pandemic situation.

How is the globalist agenda imposed?

After what was seen in the previous chapter regarding the great icons of the globalist agenda, the answer to how the globalist agenda is imposed is easy and it is basically done in two ways.

The first is thanks to the concentration of the media that we have just mentioned.

Second, thanks to the action of the icons of the globalist agenda, and to the action and dispositions emanating from supranational entities not democratically elected that we mentioned in the previous chapter.

The Globalist Agenda in the 21st Century: The Great Reset

What is the Big Reboot or Reset?

The Great Reset is a program of world change or restart that includes political, economic and social areas at a global level promoted by the World Economic Forum that meets once a year almost always in the city of Davos, Switzerland, and in which the pandemic of Covid-19 is precisely used as an excuse to promote these changes. This is how the president and founder of the World Economic Forum, Klaus Schwab, expresses it in his book "Covid-19: The Great Reset" published in June 2020: The pandemic represents a rare but narrow window of opportunity to reflect, reimagine, and reset our world to create a healthier, more equitable, and more prosperous future."

What are the objectives of the International Economic Forum?

Although these are collected in various articles on its website, they are summarized in a short video of just over a minute about eight predictions for the world in 2030. Obviously it is not only predictions but they are a faithful reflection of the objectives of the globalist agenda, which the World Economic Forum wants to impose. These predictions/goals are:

1. "You will have nothing and you will be happy. You can rent things that you need and a drone will take you home. "That is, the end of capitalism and the return to socialism as an imposed world economic system are promoted, in which, as in any socialist system, there will be a tax increase of progressive nature, that is, the rich pay a higher percentage of taxes than the poor, with a consequent redistribution of wealth and resources, with which everyone will end up having the same economic capacity and resources, except the rulers who will be the rich. In addition, private property will be eliminated, because thanks to the technological revolution typical of the fourth industrial revolution, it will be possible to rent almost anything that a person needs and it will not be essential to own anything.

2. "The United States will not be the world's main superpower", which is almost a reality in 2021, because China is practically already economically so, which as of September

2018 was the world's largest exporter (and continues to be so in 2021) with 2.26 trillion (millions of millions) dollars compared to 1.54 trillion US dollars, that is, 32% higher export earnings, thus being the first world factory as we can see with the large number of products that we can buy in our countries and that are made in China.

3. "You will not die waiting for an organ donor": they will be manufactured with 3D printers, which is very positive if it occurs, and is in line with the technological revolution of the current fourth industrial revolution

4. "You will eat much less meat": meat will be "an occasional treat, not every day food, for the sake of the environment and our health." The defense of the environment against man-made action that causes climate change, global warming and the disappearance of resources is introduced again. Then man becomes the great enemy of man himself because he destroys the planet and destroys natural resources, and thus nature becomes a new divinity that must be venerated and protected as in pagan religions.

5. "One billion (1,000 million) people will have to be displaced by climate change. We will have to do a better job of welcoming and integrating these refugees." Thus, it is confirmed that in less than 10 years, one billion people will migrate, which is in line with the globalist dogma of mass and uncontrolled migration and the open borders policy of George Soros.

6. "Polluters will have to pay to emit carbon dioxide" - "There will be a global price for carbon. This will help make fossil fuels history. "That is, with the excuse of man-made climate change, the economic growth of poor countries that want to get out of poverty will be limited.

7. "Scientists are working towards a healthy stay in space, which can facilitate research." That is, there are too many people on this planet for the existing resources, and therefore it is necessary to live on other planets.

8. "Western values will be put to the test. The values that sustain our democracies must be considered." In other words, we must go from a capitalist economic system to a socialist one imposed by the supranational world elites, and we must allow the democracies that rule the Western nations to be replaced by a new imposed and anti-democratic world government.

It only remains to add that the problem with this world socialist system is that although it pretends to be fair and redistributive of wealth between rich and poor, the truth is that it makes the majority of people poorer, since everybody must have the same or very similar capital income and material resources, instead of allowing those who work more or have more capacity to earn more. That is, equality in itself is not fair, since for example, in which system would you prefer to live: in one where we all have to live in houses of 80 square meters or in one where we can live the majority in houses of 100 to 500 square meters according to purchasing power, even if there are some wealthy people who live in mansions of 4,000 square meters?

Resistance to the globalist agenda

It is precisely the most unpopular and patriotic politicians, often located on the political right, who are the great opponents of the globalist agenda, as It is the case with these three Protestant or evangelical presidents: the former president of the United States till January 2021, Donald Trump, Jair Bolsonaro in Brazil and Viktor Orbán in Hungary. Russian President Vladimir Putin or Chinese President Xi Jinping also strongly oppose to the globalist agenda.

In Spain, it seems quite evident that the only known political force that seems to oppose to the globalist agenda is the right-wing patriotic party Vox.

Dogma 1 of the globalist agenda:

global warming or climate change

The theory of global warming, currently called climate change, is one in which scientists and the media say that the temperature on the earth's surface is rising excessively and dangerously due to the man-made emission of greenhouse gases such as carbon dioxide (CO_2), nitrous oxide (N_2O), methane (CH_4) and ozone (O_3), of which carbon dioxide is considered to be the main cause of this greenhouse effect.

As a greenhouse effect we understand the accumulation of these gases in the atmosphere that absorb and emit radiation within the infrared range.

Thus, the theory of global warming is widely known by everybody due to its repeated and constant publication in the official media, both on television, radio and on the written press, which has made it a widely believed theory and accepted as true by the majority of the non-scientific population.

But we must not confuse the real fact that throughout the history of our planet there have been climatic changes through the centuries, and that there have always been times with warmer temperatures than others, with the fact that these observed changes in the 20th and 21st centuries are abnormal and dangerous for planet Earth. In fact, the climate is not always the same but changing and It depends on multiple factors. No one doubts, for example, that the pollution and destruction of natural habitats caused by humans has a certain environmental impact. However, this impact on the environment is widely exaggerated or falsified as we will see in this chapter.

In addition, as climate change is something complex to understand, for which knowledge is necessary to have in various scientific disciplines such as geology, physics, chemistry, etc., it is not a theory that can really question the rest of the non-scientific population to the scientists. But despite this reality and to the surprise of many people, there is a large group of scientists who prove that the theory of global warming caused by humans or dangerous climate change is not true, and that it seems that these scientifics would be wrong on this theory consciously, because they are servants of the dogmas imposed by the globalist agenda.

The dogma of dangerous climate change is what the World Economic Forum uses as an excuse to promote a political, economic and social reset, that is, we must pollute less and do everything while respecting more the environment with green policies and using renewable energy, which It is obvious that it does not justify enough any world great reset.

But the Covid-19 pandemic is also presented as an opportunity to fight against climate change. While it is true that all crises are an opportunity to change and improve, it is difficult to find the relationship between the Covid-19 pandemic and the fight against climate change. That is, any excuse is used to combat the supposed dangerous and abnormal man-made climate change.

This is what Mark Lynas explains in an article on the International Economic Forum website entitled: "COVID-19 has thrown a life guard to our planet to fight climate change."

• COVID-19 has brought climate and economic imperatives closer than ever.

• If the world seizes this opportunity, future generations will remember 2020 as the year humanity defeated a pandemic and saved the planet.

• COVID-19 killed more than 500,000 people worldwide, sickened millions and continues to wreak havoc. But, as the saying goes - and without trying to minimize this human tragedy in any way - there is no harm that does not come from good (this saying means that negative circumstances can be used for good). If we make the right decisions as lockdowns ease, perhaps the pandemic has extended a hand to humanity in dealing with the much greater challenge of climate change.

So, in summary, the great enemy with which we must fight is humanity itself that pollutes the atmosphere and causes climate change, and according to the World Economic Forum, the Covid-19 pandemic has simply made this more evident. This is a problem because with the confinement of people due to the pandemic in 2020 and the closure of many factories and businesses, much less greenhouse gases have been emitted, and cleaner skies and less polluted atmospheres have been observed. But the fact that the atmosphere has been less polluted by the confinements and the cessation of the economic activity at a global level does not indicate that climate change is the most important danger that humanity is facing and to justify a Great Reset at all levels, and more so when green and environmental policies have already been applied for decades in an increasingly growing way in most nations of the world.

Why if there is an increase in temperatures on the earth's surface or climate change is taking place, it is not dangerous?.

In the following chapters on climate change I draw on evidence presented by the International Non-Governmental Panel on Climate Change or NIPCC for its acronym, which can be found on their report, the second edition of which was published in 2014 and entitled "Why scientists disagree about global warming. The NIPCC Report on Scientific Consensus ".

The key findings of this book include the following:

There is no scientific consensus as the most important fact about climate science, which is often overlooked, is that scientists disagree on the environmental impacts of burning fossil fuels on the global climate.

Thus the articles and surveys most frequently cited in support of the "scientific consensus" in favor of dangerous global warming hypotheses are without exception, methodologically flawed, and often deliberately misleading.

In fact, there is no survey or study that shows "consensus" on the most important aspects and scientific issues in the climate change debate, and numerous survey data shows deep disagreement among scientists on scientific questions that must be resolved before the hypothesis of man-made global warming caused be validated.

Importantly, many leading experts and probably most working scientists disagree with the claims made by the United Nations Intergovernmental Panel on Climate Change (IPCC).

Why Scientists Disagree

Climate is an interdisciplinary subject that requires knowledge from many fields of study. Very few scholars are proficient in more than one or two of these disciplines and fundamental uncertainties arise from insufficient observation of the evidence, from disagreements on how to interpret the data, and how to set the parameters in climatological models.

The IPCC was created to find and disseminate research that finds a human impact on the global climate, so It is not a credible source. It is driven by an agenda, and it is more of a political body than a scientific one, and many say corrupt.

Thus scientists who study climate, like all humans, can be biased, and the origins of these biases are often found in pursuit of their career advancement, in pursuit of grants, in political pressures and biases of confirmation of the information.

Is there really a consensus of 97% of global scientists that climate change is human-caused, urgent and dangerous?

The full story can be found on the YouTube video called "The in-depth story behind a climate fraud" investigated and narrated by Dr. John Robson, who is the executive director of the Climate Discussion Nexus, and whose link I share in the bibliography at the end of the book:

So in 2009 a pair of researchers from the University of Illinois sent an online survey to more than 10,000 scientists who were studying the planet Earth, asking two simple questions: "Do you agree that global temperatures have generally risen since before 1800? "and" Do you think human activity is a significant contributing factor to this? " [Note: they also asked some other questions, but did not report the questions or results in the publication].

The survey did not mention greenhouse gases, did not explain what the term "significant" meant and did not mention the danger or climate crisis. So what was the result?.

Of the 3,146 responses they received, 90 percent said yes to the first question, meaning that global temperatures had risen since the Little Ice Age, and only 82 percent said yes to the second, that activity human was a significant contributing factor.

Interestingly, among meteorologists, only 64 percent said yes to the second question, meaning that a third of the experts in the study of weather patterns who answered did not believe that humans played a significant role in global warming, much less a dominant one.

What most caught the media's attention was that among the 77 respondents who described themselves as climate experts, 75 said yes to the second question. 75 of 77 is 97%.

Exactly, It did not attract the attention of the media that they only took 77 of the 3,146 responses. But that's the key statistical trick. They found a 97 percent consensus among 2 percent of those surveyed. And yet this consensus was only on the fact that there had been some warming since the 19th century, which virtually no one denies, and that humans are partly responsible. These experts did not say that warming was dangerous or urgent, because they were not asked. [Note: or as stated above, if they were actually asked if warming was dangerous or urgent, the results did not report on it].

Therefore so far, the claim that 97% of "world scientists" say that there is a climate crisis is pure fiction.

Scientific method versus political science

The implicit assumption in all IPCC writing, though rarely explicitly stated, is that dangerous global warming is the result, or will be the result, of human-related greenhouse gas emissions.

The null hypothesis that is implicitly denied is that currently observed changes in global climate indices and in the physical environment, as well as current changes in animal and plant characteristics, are the result of natural variability.

Thus, in contradiction to the scientific method, the IPCC implicitly assumes that their hypothesis is correct and that their only duty is to collect evidence and make plausible arguments in favor of the hypothesis.

Flawed projections

The IPCC and virtually all governments in the world rely on global climate models (GCM) to forecast the effects of greenhouse gas emissions on the climate.

Global climate models systematically overestimate the sensitivity of the climate to carbon dioxide (CO_2), many known causes and feedbacks are poorly modelled, and the modelers exclude causes and feedbacks that go against their mission of finding human influence on the climate.

Additionally, four specific forecasts made by global climate models have been falsified by real-world data from a wide variety of sources. In particular, it has been proven that there has been no global warming for about 18 years from September 1996 to September 2014

False postulates

Neither the rate nor the magnitude of the reports on warming on the Earth's surface in the latter part of the 20th century (1979-2000) are outside normal natural variability.

The warm spike of the late 20th century was no greater in magnitude than previous spikes caused entirely by natural causes and feedbacks.

Also historically, increases in atmospheric CO_2 followed, not preceded, increases in temperature. Therefore, the CO_2 levels cannot have caused the temperatures to rise.

Solar factors are not too small and insignificant to explain 20th century warming. In fact, its effect could be equal to or greater than the effect of CO2 in the atmosphere.

Thus a warming of 2 ° C or more during the 21st century is probably not harmful, because many areas of the world would benefit or adapt to climate change, and in colder areas new vegetation would grow and cereals, fruit trees and plants could be cultivated which would not grow in a colder climate.

Unreliable circumstantial evidence

The melting of Arctic sea ice and the polar ice caps does not occur at "unnatural" rates and is not evidence of a human impact on the climate.

In this way the best available data shows that sea level rise is not accelerating. Local and regional sea levels continue to exhibit typical natural variability, rising in some places and decreasing in others. Furthermore, the relationship between warming and drought is weak and according to some measured data, drought decreased during the 20th century. In fact, changes in the hydrosphere (part of the Earth occupied by oceans, seas, rivers, lakes and other water bodies and currents) of this type are regionally highly variable and show a closer correlation with climatic rhythmicity in several decades than with global temperature.

Nor has a convincing relationship been established between global warming in the last 100 years and the increase in extreme weather events. In fact, meteorological science suggests just the opposite: a warmer world causes milder weather patterns.

There is no evidence that current changes in the Arctic permafrost (soil layer permanently frozen, but not permanently covered with ice or snow in very cold or periglacial regions) are not simply natural, or are likely to cause a climate catastrophe by releasing methane into the atmosphere.

Political implications

Rather than relying exclusively on the IPCC for scientific advice, policymakers should seek the advice of independent non-governmental organizations and scientists who are free from financial and political conflicts of interest.

Thus individual nations should be responsible for establishing their own policies based on the risks that apply to their particular geography, geology, climate and culture.

On the other hand, instead of investing the scarce world resources in a huge campaign based on politicized and unreliable science, national leaders would do well to focus their attention on the real problems facing their people and their planet.

Summary of NIPCC findings on Physical Science

1. Atmospheric carbon dioxide (CO_2) is a mild greenhouse gas that exerts a decreasing warming effect as its concentration increases.

2. Doubling the concentration of atmospheric CO2 from its pre-industrial level, in the absence of other variables and feedbacks, would probably cause a warming of -0.3 ° C to 1.1 ° C, almost 50 percent of what must have already occurred.

So a few tenths of a degree of additional warming, should it occur, does not represent a climate crisis.

3. The results of the models published in successive IPCC reports since 1990, project that a doubling of CO2 could cause a warming of up to 6 ° C by 2100. In contrast, global warming ceased at the end of the 20th century and was followed since 1997 by 18 years of stable temperature.

4. During recent geological time, the Earth's temperature has naturally fluctuated between approximately + 4 ° C and -6 ° C in relation to the temperature of the 20th century. A warming of 2 ° C in temperature above the current temperature, if it occurred, would be within the limits of natural variability.

5. Although a future warming of 2 ° C would cause various ecological responses, there is no evidence that these changes are clearly detrimental to the global environment or to human well-being.

6. At the current level of 400 ppm (400 parts of carbon dioxide per one million parts of air), we still live in a world that needs more CO2. During the Cambrian period, CO_2 atmospheric levels existed 15 times higher (about 550 million years ago) with no known adverse effects.

7. The general warming since approximately 1860 corresponds to a recovery from the Little Ice Age, modulated by natural cycles lasting several decades driven by ocean-atmospheric oscillations, or by variations in solar radiation cycles called Vries (approximately 208 years long) and Gleissberg (approximately 80 years long) and for shorter periods as well.

8. The Earth has not warmed significantly over the past 18 years despite an 8 percent increase in atmospheric CO2, which accounts for 34 percent of all extra CO_2 added to the atmosphere since the start of the industrial revolution.

9. There is no close correlation between temperature variation in the last 150 years and human-related CO_2 emissions. The parallelism of the increase in temperature and CO2 between 1980 and 2000 AD could therefore be due to chance and does not necessarily indicate causality.

10. The causes of historical global warming remain uncertain, but there are significant correlations between weather patterns, variation over several decades, and solar activity over the last few hundred years.

11. Future projections of solar cycles imply that the coming decades will be marked by global cooling rather than warming, despite continued CO2 emissions.

<u>Historical evidence that current global warming is not abnormal or dangerous</u>

If we are really experiencing global warming, which is debatable especially considering the severe winter 2020-2021 with heavy snowfalls that we are experiencing in the Northern Hemisphere, this is not the first time that it has occurred in the history of this planet. Thus there have been earlier times of global warming according to known historical accounts:

Times of global warming greater than the current one:

1. Final period of the glaciations.

2. Mycenaean period, that is, in the period coinciding with the Trojan War.

3. First century BC coinciding with the time of Julius Caesar and the Gallic War.

4. The Middle Ages

5. The 1930s.

All except the 1930s are times when there were no automobiles, factories or industries, so it is quite obvious that global warming temperatures in those times were not man-made, and that the reason was natural and above all related to the sun and its radiation cycles.

In addition, there have also been failed predictions related to global warming and climate change in the last 50 years:

- 1967: "Terrible famine for 1975"

- 1969: "All will disappear in a cloud of blue vapor by 1989"

- 1970: "Ice Age in 2000"

- 1970: "America will suffer water rationing in 1974 and food rationing in 1980"

- 1974: The ozone hole is a "great danger to life"

- 1980: "Acid rain kills life in lakes"

- 1988: The Maldives will be underwater in 30 years

- 1989: Sea level rise will "destroy" most countries by the year 2000

- 2000: "Children will not know what snow is"

- 2004: Britain will have Siberian weather by 2020

- 2008: The Arctic will run out of ice by 2018

- 2009: The Arctic will run out of ice by 2014

- 2013: The Arctic will run out of ice by 2015

- 2014: Only 500 days to go before "climate chaos"

Today, in 2021, the deception continues ...

NASA's Role in Global Warming Theory

NASA, which is lhe National Aeronautics and Space Administration of the United States of America, is also one of the promoters of the theory of dangerous global warming or dangerous climate change. In fact, its reputation is known worldwide not only for placing the first men on the moon with the Apollo 11 spacecraft on July 20, 1969, but also for the multitude of American films where this agency appears performing all kinds of missions. Thus NASA is also in charge of publishing infinity of data on temperatures on the earth's surface or in the atmosphere, or of all kinds of climatological data where indeed the data seem to prove that there is global warming. In addition they also publish many graphs with this data,

Despite this, it should be noted that although there is actually an increase in the earth's temperature since the middle of the 20th century, this does not mean that it is dangerous for the survival of the planet or that it is occurring in an unnatural way. So the same happens with most weather phenomena, which although they actually occur, it is by no means proven that they are occurring in an unnatural way, unlike other periods in history.

In addition, the measured data presented by NASA regarding the climate are from the 20th and 21st centuries and not from previous centuries in order to be able to accurately compare them with other times in history, since NASA was created on October 1, 1958, which represents a great limitation, since then the calculations of temperatures from times prior to the 20th century must be made based on estimates, based on climatological models whose parameters can easily be wrong or manipulated.

It should also be noted that NASA is a public agency paid exclusively by the American State, so it will supposedly provide data and explanations of these data according to the official theory on the climate maintained by the United States government, so It would make sense to doubt about its impartiality regarding what the NASA may say on this issue, as well about the impartiality regarding what the UN Intergovernmental Panel on Climate Change (IPCC) may say about global warming.

Greta Thunberg & Co.

Today it seems that the globalist agenda has among its objectives the recruitment, use and abuse of children and teenagers like Greta Thunberg. This teenager today has become at the age of 18, one of the best known faces of the defense against climate change and the theory of global warming.

In a recent speech to the United Nation, she accused world leaders of having stolen his dreams and childhood and said: "We are at the beginning of mass extinction and all they talk about is money and fairy tales about eternal economic growth. ". In addition, together with fifteen other children, he filed a formal complaint before the United Nations Committee in charge of the rights of the child, which accuses Argentina, Germany, France, Brazil and Turkey of violating the rights of children by not taking sufficient care of global warming. The funny thing is that they did not mention China, India or the United States for example, which are among the largest polluters on the planet.

Unfortunately, Greta's speeches often border on the tone of hatred, and she is increasingly provoking negative reactions from world leaders. So even Angela Merkel, who originally praised her, said that Greta had not spoken correctly because today technology and innovation, especially in the energy conservation sector, expand the possibilities to achieve protection goals of the environment and climate change.

Human practices of climate modification

In fact, the modification of the climate by humans is not something new, and in an open way it has been experimented and used by nations such as the United States for its strategic use in wars, as for example it was done in the Vietnam War by this nation. Thus, the American journalist Seymour Hersh revealed in 1972 that the United States tried to manipulate the seasonal rains during the Vietnam War in what was called Operation Popeye, with the aim of flooding the communist route along the route of the leader Ho Chi Minh. The technology was later adopted and improved by the Soviet Union and fervently applied by China during the so-called "Great Leap Forward", when Mao Zedong said "man-made rain is very important".

Apparently the human modification of the climate by China has been peaceful and for domestic use, so for example in northern China this climate change is coordinated by the Beijing climate modification office, which claims to have increased precipitation in the capital of the Chinese nation by more than 10%. For example, it was claimed that these weather modification practices helped alleviate a prolonged drought, and that before the 2008 Olympics more than 1,000 silver iodide shells were thrown into the sky for more than eight hours to keep the rain from interrupting the opening ceremony of the Olympic Games.

This technology has also been used to clear smoke from the atmosphere ahead of the 2014 Asia-Pacific Economic Cooperation meeting.

Thus, in China, climate modification is institutionalized and widely used, and the application of solar radiation management measures is even being considered. But obviously there are dangers to the extent to which the Chinese Communist Government wishes to go with the manipulation of the elements that affect the climate. So in 1970 Chinese generals proposed using nuclear weapons to create a channel through the Himalayas, so that warm, humid air from the Indian subcontinent could be diverted to grow vegetated areas in the deserts of northern and central China. In addition, the Chinese nation is also in the middle of the world's largest water diversion program, whose goal is similar. However, many scientists, even within China, have doubts about the effectiveness and good intentions of artificial cloud creation programs, particularly on a large scale, as they can obviously easily be used by China to create a climate war favorable to the interests of the Chinese communist regime against other nations

Just before writing these lines, I read that John Rendon, the CEO and president of The Rendon Group (TRG), which is an American strategic communications consulting firm, being also John Rendon in the past CEO and political director of the Democratic Party of The United States, said this on its Twitter account on January 6, 2021: The Nordic regions of America, Asia and Europe should prepare for erratic and episodic weather events this winter. In other words, in the northern hemisphere we are going to have a hard winter, due to the fact that the polar vertex, understanding as a polar vertex according to Wikipedia, a large-scale persistent cyclone located near the terrestrial polar areas, which are also located in the middle and upper troposphere and in the stratosphere, it is weakening and reeling caused by a "sudden" warming event in the stratosphere. The funny thing is that this event occurs suddenly as if it appeared out of nowhere and for no reason, which obviously implies that it may be the result of human climate manipulation.

Shortly after the Russian sources of www.whatdoesitmean.com publish that it has been the Chinese government that has prepared this climate war that is giving us a freezing winter.

Latest personal experience on climate change

I have lived in Barcelona, Spain, for most of my life, which is over 40 years now, and the truth is that the summer of 2020 has not been the hottest, not even close, nor have there been as many heat waves as in previous years. Also, this autumn andwinter of 2020-2021 are being much colder than in previous years at least here in Spain. So as I write in the city of Barcelona we are at 5ºC, which is a fairly low temperature in a humid Mediterranean climate like Barcelona, and there has been heavy snowfalls in most of Spain. In fact, since the beginning of October 2020 I have worn a winter jacket almost every day, while in previous years there have been weeks of relative heat in October. In short, it does not seem to me that temperatures have risen at all in 2020-2021 in the northern hemisphere and specifically in Spain where I live.

Dogma 2 of the globalist agenda: massive and uncontrolled migration

Although orderly and controlled migration in many cases can bring economic growth in the countries that receive it, for example with the fact that many immigrants dare to undertake and open new businesses that the local inhabitants do not usually dare to open, since generally immigrants have a greater tendency to start new businesses, due to among other factors because they are people who have come from another country and have already had to take risks in many situations before, therefore having a lower fear to taking risks.

Thus, although it is logical, understandable and humane for people to seek new destinations with new homes where they can increase their quality of life, it is also necessary to remember that for example the Roman Empire collapsed among other reasons because it did not know or could not control its borders well. In other words, a good orderly border control is necessary to maintain national integrity and security.

However, both George Soros and the globalist agenda defend a very lax border control and migration policy, which is defended by practically all international supranational entities such as the UN. The objective of advocating for a massive and uncontrolled migration is none other than to gradually erode the cultural and identity values of sovereign nations, so that little by little it may be easier to empty them of power and they may be more easily controllable from globalist entities.

Thus, on July 13, 2018, the Global Pact on Migration was agreed in Marrakech, Morocco, which although it may seem full of good intentions, is supported by the objectives of the globalist agenda, since it appeals to a multilateral governance system such as the UN , being the threat of climate change mentioned in It. Thus, the Spanish Minister of Foreign Affairs, European Union and Communication, Josep Borrell, wrote in an article of December 12, 2018 on the website of the Ministry of Foreign Affairs of the Spanish Government like this:

"The world is a common and shared space, in which permanent interconnection and communication and transport technologies generate flows of people, goods, information and ideas on a scale that was unimaginable until recently. This requires a system of multilateral governance, which is what the UN was born for at the end of World War II and in full discredit of nationalisms, which even today have not quite left the scene.

Population movements are a natural, secular, and structural phenomenon, which is neither an anomaly nor a threat, and will therefore remain on the political agenda for decades to come. A challenge that can only be addressed through international cooperation. No country, not even a region, can manage it alone. Its nature is intrinsically transnational, as is the challenge of climate change, a factor that also influences the displacement of people, as a consequence of desertification, together with insecurity, poverty or the simple lack of opportunities. And, as the UN Secretary General has recalled, no one can really be surprised that human beings seek a better future for themselves and their families. "

Although it is obviously not surprising that human beings move to seek a better future, it is not surprising either that since August 2020 boats have arrived in the Canary Islands like never before with precisely immigrants from Morocco and North Africa, who have been transferred to hotel complexes to accommodate them, since many of these are documented inmigrants unlike Africans from sub-Saharan Africa, and even the undocumented immigrants roamed the streets with complete freedom. In an article in the digital newspaper "el Confidencial" dated from October 31, 2020, it said the following: "This wave of crowded boats (up to 150 people per boat) arriving incessantly to the Canary Islands since August It is generating a lot of social confusion. The feeling is very different from the crisis of the "cayucos" (small boats) of 2006, when 515 boats arrived in the Canary Islands with 31,678 people on board, almost all from sub-Saharan African countries plagued by war and poverty. Then, the immigrants were put on buses and taken to military installations to proceed with their identification and subsequent deportation, or to relocate them to Spanish territory if they met the conditions of asylum.

This time, immigrants are referred to touristic accommodations, where they have complete freedom of movement despite not having an identity document in many cases. The daily sight of large groups of people wandering the streets of southern Gran Canaria, in high value tourist enclaves such as Maspalomas and Puerto Rico, has given rise to great social unrest."

Dogma 3 of the globalist agenda: gender ideology

The gender ideology, that is, the right that gender is not defined by nature itself but by what the person feels or thinks has been a reality for decades.

The gender ideology also seems to have managed to be accepted even among many christian sectors, and to have managed to silence practically everyone, even ecclesial bodies like those of the Vatican.

Thus, gender ideology tries to explain that nature does not determine the sex or gender of a person, and that the term man or woman has been used based on the male and female genitalia as an excuse to create a system of oppression of the heterosexual men or patriarchy against women and homosexual men and women, trans or of any other type of fluid gender (gender changing). It is therefore a conception of class struggle with oppressors and oppressed similar to the theory of the Communist Manifesto of Karl Marx and Friedrich Engels, but using the sex and gender of people as a starting point.

In any case, it is respectable that people can agree with the gender ideology, but it is undeniable that there is a progressive imposition of this ideology in the laws, in education, etc., since less and less parents can educate their children in the religion, philosophy or ideology that they want, but they have to forcibly accept the vision of gender ideology that is imposed on their children in the classrooms, as It happens for example with the recently approved in December 2020, "Ley Celá" (Celá Law) in Spain, named after Isabel Celá, Minister of Education and Vocational Training of the Spanish Government. This imposition of the gender ideology by the entities and elites that organize the globalist agenda, often conditions the granting of economic aid to the governments of nations in exchange for their supporting of this ideology through the creation of laws in favor of It, for example, and the consequent legalization of its principles.

In fact, gender ideology is always defended as a human right, but its imposition against the will of the parents of children in school classrooms and of people in general violates the human rights of these people.

Like any other dogma of the globalist agenda, it is defended by any supranational entity such as the UN, the World Health Organization, the International Economic Forum, the Bilderberg Club, etc.

Indeed, the ultimate goal of promoting the gender ideology is to dissociate and displace the family as the basic social nucleus in society, which has been the typically Christian basic nucleus of Western societies for centuries, in order to gradually create a society with others moral values, more secular and capable of being shaped by globalist elites, and of course preventing population growth which is something that families do.

So we must remember that the directors of financial, technological, media, big pharmaceutical companies, etc. who are in the supranational organizations of the globalist agenda are not particularly interested in the rights of LGTBIQ + people but in controlling the destinies of the world population, of which David Rockefeller is a faithful reflection, for example, as stated in his book "Memories" published in 2002, and what can be achieved through gender ideology for the globalist objectives.

Dogma 4 of the globalist agenda: extreme feminism

In fact, it is closely related to gender ideology, promoting the idea that men have historically oppressed women, and that they have held positions of power in which women were absent due to a "macho" and patriarchal culture, which it has been true in many eras and in many societies throughout history.

But in the present Western extreme feminist current, for example in most of the countries of the European Union, the man is presented as the culprit of almost all the problems of women, and it is even legislated against men and in favor of women in countries like Spain, on issues that have to do with domestic violence, child custody, etc. That is, for example, that if a woman denounces a man for mistreatment or domestic violence, it is understood that the woman is telling the truth and it is not necessary to prove it, so immediately in many cases the man is arrested and put in the police cell for the protection of the woman, against the presumption of innocence that should govern in Western law.

Also, for example, according to Spanish gender legislation, in the face of equal conditions for a father and a mother, custody of children in the event of separation or divorce is always granted preferably to the woman rather than to the man.

And for example in Spain if it is proved that a woman has falsely denounced a man for gender or domestic violence, the woman is not penalized or fined later for it.

In fact, this extreme feminism supported by legislation in favor of women and against men, and in the case of Spain as well supported by even a Ministry of Equality, which is rather unnecessary, since unlike what has happened historically, women in most Western democratic nations have enjoyed practically the same rights as men for decades, and also have special legislation and entities that defend women's rights.

It is precisely in Western democratic nations where more feminist movements in favor of women's rights and against men take place, while nevertheless the rights and freedoms of women have not only been equaled to those of men, but also in addition, they have in many cases exceeded those of men.

Obviously, this extreme feminism is also driven by the globalist agenda to undermine and erode the family as a basic social nucleus and to confront men and women, producing a tension within the nations, which is favorable to the objectives of the globalist agenda, eroding not only the social nucleus of the traditional family but also democracies themselves, while the globalist elites have with these tensions and confrontations a new excuse to be able to meddle in national politics.

Dogma 5 of the globalist agenda: abortion

The worldwide advance in the legalization of abortion has been constant since the 1970s. In fact, since then it is considered that there have been some 1.4 billion (1,400 million) abortions worldwide since today.

In fact, although the heart of a human fetus begins to beat for the first time after three weeks, today in many nations abortions are practiced during any period of gestation, and there are even abortions after having given birth.

Abortion is justified by saying that fetuses are not yet human, but the worldwide spreaded USA organization "Planned Parenthood", whose main source of business is abortion and not exactly family planning in the broad sense, sells aborted fetuses to laboratories to do their experiments, which shows that fetuses are considered human by "Planned Parenthood" itself.

In addition, although abortion allows skipping the pregnancy and the subsequent care and education of the baby, it is not usually said that abortion leaves psychological and emotional consequences for the mother, in what is known as post-abortion syndrome (for example, sense of guilt, sadness, depression), in addition to in quite a number of cases bleeding problems for weeks.

In fact, abortion is not the only solution to an unexpected pregnancy, because there are associations that offer counseling and help to mothers during and after pregnancy, informing about public or private aid for maternity, as in the case in Spain of the Red Foundation Mother.

In any case, on the website of the United Nation, the World Health Organization and most of the supranational entities that support the globalist agenda, they promote abortion as if it were the only solution to unexpected pregnancies, although abortion is not in fact the best solution for mother's health. Thus, the promotion and sponsorship of abortion responds to the Malthusian idea of reducing the world population, so that a smaller number of population can be more easily controlled by these supranational globalist instances.

Curiously, the trend of legalization of abortion in different countries is that it can increasingly be practiced at any time of pregnancy and not only in the first four months and for any reason, not just in case of rape or risk of death for the mother. Thus, this unconditionality of the practice of abortion is even more extreme than the legislation that the Nazis had for it, who only practiced it in cases of genetic problems of the fetus or in case of risk to the mother's health or life.

Dogma 6 of the globalist agenda: euthanasia

Euthanasia, like abortion, has its antecedents in the eugenic policies of the Nazis of the 20th century. Eugenics was the application of the biological laws of heredity and genetic modification in order to improve the human species, based on a presumed superiority of the Aryan or Northern European race over all others.

Thus, in order to improve the human species, euthanasia was applied to children and people with terminal illnesses or genetic defects, along with abortion.

Today the legalization of euthanasia is spreading in more and more countries and is increasingly permitted in more cases, especially in terminally ill patients. In fact, several media outlets expressed that the tens of thousands of deaths in 2020 of isolated elderly people in nursing homes in Spain, who died more from personal and health neglect than from the Covid-19 virus Itself, with the excuse that they could infect health workers and family members. Thus, they were isolated in such a way that their relatives could not visit them nor were they really given the necessary health care, in what appears to be an exercise of generalized euthanasia and population reduction in harmony with globalist population reduction dogmas and objectives. For example, the Vitalia Leganés nursing home, ne of the largest in the private sector in Madrid, recognized that as of April 2, 2020, that is at the beginning of the pandemic, more than 89 people had already died of Covid-19 according to the families of the victims. Curiously, the current first vice president of the Spanish government, Pablo Iglesias, of the left-wing communist party, Unidas Podemos, had sole command of the management of nursing homes at that time.

Dogma 7 of the globalist agenda: the legalization of drug trafficking, trade and consumption

Thus, George Soros himself, since 1992, has defended the legalization of drug trafficking, trade and consumption, claiming that it is a human right, and that legalization would end the devastating effects that produces on the economy of nations the illegal drug trafficking and trade, along with the increase in crime related to drug trafficking, and the devastating effect it has on the health and death of many users. But in fact, the same as if, for example, the rapes of women and children were legalized from 10 p.m. to 11 p.m. on Saturday nights in order to put an end to the rapes would not finish with the problem, nor the partial or total legalization of drug trafficking and trade would finish with this problem.

In fact, drug trafficking and trade is a plague as evidenced by the historical experiences of the large drug cartels, for example in Colombia and Mexico, and therefore to end such a big problem it is necessary to regulate and control it, including in addition to adequate legislation in this regard, greater and more effective police control and better border control between countries.

Thus, the legalization of drug trafficking, trade and consumption simply causes greater social problems in nations, including broken families, so it is not surprising that among the globalist agenda the massive legalization of drugs is one of its dogmas in order to subvert the national order, and have an excuse to impose a new supranational world order that also would control the borders.

The great friendship between the Great Reset and Covid-19

Much has been debated in 2020 about whether the Covid-19 virus is of natural origin or created and modified in the laboratory. Although in fact it is a good debate, it can be a bit useless, because whether we are facing a natural virus or a laboratory created virus, we are going to have to face it anyway. But if something does not admit doubt, it is that as the financial newspaper "Financial Times" and many experts said in 2019 through platforms such as YouTube, by 2020-2021 an economic, political and social great reset would come, which is already taking place and that has It was announced and explained by the World Economic Forum in 2020 on its own website, and whose meeting in May 2021 in Singapur is going to be titled precisely "Great Reset" dealing with this topic.

Therefore, it is more logical to think that this virus was created in a laboratory in order to use it to create a great global reset, than to think that the greatest coincidence in history has occurred, coinciding by hazard a previously announced large reset with a new pandemic. In other words, it is a very large coincidence that precisely in 2020 the previously announced Great Reset coincides with a pandemic that still lasts in 2021.

So without a doubt, the Covid-19 pandemic is being used to advance the globalist agenda, make a great psychological experiment with confinements and see how far people resist, as stated on the same website of the World Economic Forum in a article dated as of April 9th 2020 entitled "Confinement is the world's greatest psychological experiment, and we will pay the price for it." Thus, with the fear induced with the help of the mass media that continuously are talking about infected people and deaths from the virus, it is possible to better control people, who are willing to sacrifice their rights and freedoms in exchange for supposed protection, security and care allegedly provided by the governements of the nations.

In addition, after the pandemic was officially declared by the World Health Organization in early March 2020, in practically all the countries of the world we have been experiencing restrictions on mobility, confinement and using masks. The truth is that as of January 2021, that is, more than 10 months later, it has been proven that the confinements and the use of masks at most produce a decrease and relief in the case of temporary infections and deaths from Covid-19, which increases again when restriction measures are relaxed, and that the Covid-19 virus does not disappear in summer when temperatures rise. So more than ever the world seem to wander aimlessly, since first the mass media said that once there was a vaccine, restrictions and confinements could be relaxed and the pandemic would end, but now there are already several vaccines against Covid-19 on the market, whose creation and investigation has been extremely, from various pharmaceutical companies, which do not appear to be effective and are causing serious side effects and even the death among people who receive them. And second, that confinements, hygiene, security measures, and the use of masks do not seem to be enough to end the pandemic as observed in more than 10 months of the supposed "plandemic".Third, that the virus can mutate at any time, as it seems to have happened with the new UK strain that appeared at the end of 2020, and these vaccines released in such a hurry and which are producing so many adverse effects when administered would be even less effective.

Fourth, that for example the flu virus itself every year we have a new vaccine because the virus mutates, and despite this the flu has never disappeared.

In short, neither confinements, nor the use of masks, nor hygiene and safety measures, etc. have been enough to contain the pandemic, but today these same measures against the virus continue to be applied continuously without knowing exactly how long for, as if they were the solution to the pandemic, while nevertheless making more hospitals and more intensive care units, training more health workers or to only confine the risk groups such as the elderly, does not seem to be in the plans of almost any government. How strange!. Isn't It?.

In this way we continue to be deprived of our rights and freedoms such as freedom of movement with the excuse of the Covid-19 pandemic, when these measures have already proved that they are not the solution, and not only we are deprived of the right to the freedom of movement but also of the right to the freedom of expression, given that since the beginning of the pandemic large technological companies (mainly the "Big Tech"), especially through their social networks, have been responsible for censoring content or dissenting opinions to the official narrative on the pandemic, censorship that has also been applied by many governments like the current Spanish social-communist government. Thus, the government of the current Spanish president Pedro Sánchez has created an organization, popularly known as the Ministry of "Truth", to monitor the alleged "false news" spread over the internet.

Thus, even after the session of January the 6th, 2021, certifying the results of the US presidential elections of November 3th, 2020 in the American Capitol, which was interrupted by the assault on it of some people, technology companies have censored and have even deleted the accounts of the then president of the United States, Donald Trump, on social networks such as Twitter, saying that he was inciting to violence through his publications and that he was responsible for organizing a mutiny to assault the US Capitol.

The first democracy and the fragility of western democracies

The first existing democracy was in Ancient Greece in the 5th and 4th centuries BC, lasting approximately a little less than two centuries, and it ended up disappearing for various reasons. One of these causes seems to be that the one who governed the people was not a person of decent or educated morals, but rather a thief and it was so because he was the most convenient person.

In addition, democracy seemed to have disappeared in Ancient Greece because the people were easily manipulated, so politicians sought to achieve and maintain power based on the popular vote and to achieve this they did not seek to do good for society but to flatter the masses, in the sense of giving to them what they asked for, may it be money, jobs, land, livestock, etc. Thus the people expected their rulers to give or grant them more and more favors instead of ruling them well.

In addition, the city-state of Athens interfered in the politics of other states such as Sparta, and this imperial vision ended up increasing military expenses, which on the other hand was well seen by the classes that lived from the war industry.

So all these factors made democracy disappear in Athens, although it would later reappear much more weakened in 399 BC with the execution of the philosopher Socrates, simply because the politicians considered honest men who spoke the truth a threat to them.

Nowadays with national governments happens similarly to what happened in the polis of Athens, so politicians make promises in electoral campaigns to win votes, and then they grant aid, privileges and favors to client networks so that these ones continue to vote for these politicians allowing them to be reelected, rather seeking to flatter the people than really to help them.

Thus, although democracy is in theory a more just political system than a dictatorship because the rulers are chosen more or less directly in elections by the people, it is nevertheless easier to maintain power in a dictatorship than in a democracy, and that is why the implantation of dictatorships with the control of the institutions and the elimination of political competition is such a great temptation for politicians in the government of a democratic system. Thus it has happened with the former president of Venezuela Hugo Chávez at the end of the 20th century and the beginning of the 21st century who was elected by an overwhelming majority in democratic elections and then little by little impose a dictatorship through the control of the country's institutions, through the control of the army and the censorship imposed on the freedom of expression.

It also happened similarly with Hitler and Mussolini who were non-internationalist nationalist socialists elected in not very clean democratic elections, and who ended up eliminating the parliamentary system and the political opposition, implanting a dictatorship.

Ultimately we see that democracy is a system that is often threatened, among other causes, by the dictatorial forces of the rulers in order to maintain their power, and in which the rulers do not usually seek the good of the general society but rather create clientelistic networks to which they grant economic aid, privileges and favors, etc., such as the concessions of public state services to certain companies, in order to continue to remain in power through their votes and support.

The Origin of Modern Democracy: The Protestant Reformation

As we have seen, Athenian democracy disappeared and did not reappear until the 16th century as a result of the Protestant reform, a reform of only spiritual matters but that indirectly introduced great changes in the nations where it was implanted.

So in summary the Roman Catholic Church had become a mixture of Greek philosophy, Roman law and pagan spirituality and had nothing to do with the early church of the first century after Christ. The Protestant Reformation brought the Bible back to being considered, as it had been in the early church, as the only God-inspired book to be studied and be considered the divine word. Thus the countries that adopted it such as Germany, the United Kingdom, the Netherlands, Switzerland, part of today's Belgium, etc. unlike the countries that did not do so and adopted the Catholic Counter-Reformation such as Spain, France, Italy, Portugal, evolved towards democratic states, since they accepted the supremacy of the law over the interpretation that the institutions gave to the law.

In addition, the Protestant Reformation also influenced the creation of the concept of public servant, of limited power of the governors, of the election of magistrates and the separation of powers to counteract abuses of the state power.

The fourth industrial revolution

Whereas at the end of the 17th century it was the steam engine, this time it seems that robots integrated into cyber-physical systems will be responsible for a radical transformation.

Economists have named it: the fourth industrial revolution that theoretically is marked by the convergence of digital, physical and biological technologies, a convergence that anticipates that the world as we know it will change.

Sounds very radical? In fact if the predictions come true, it will be. And it is happening, they say, on a large scale and at full speed.

Klaus Schwab, President of the World Economic Forum and author of the book "The Fourth Industrial Revolution" published in 2016, wrote: "We are on the brink of a technological revolution that will fundamentally change the way we live, work and interact, In its scale, scope and complexity, the transformation will be unlike anything mankind has ever experienced before ".

Thus, theoretically, in the fourth industrial revolution, manufacturing will change radically and with it the world of employment. In fact, the factories of the fourth industrial revolution seem to be automatic and very intelligent.

In fact, the "new powers" of change would come from the hand of genetic engineering and neurotechnologies, two areas that perhaps seem remote to the ordinary citizen, but whose repercussions in theory will impact how we are and how we relate, even in the farthest corners of the planet: the revolution in theory will affect the job market, the future of work, income inequality and its consequences will impact geopolitical security and ethical frameworks.

So what is the change about and why are there those who believe that it is about a revolution?

The important thing, the theorists of the idea emphasize, is that it is not about developments, but about the meeting of those developments. And in that sense, it represents a paradigm shift, rather than another step in the frenzied tech race.

So these are in theory the 5 keys to understand the REVOLUTION 4.0:

1. Germany was the first country to put it on the government agenda as a "high-tech strategy."

2. It is based on cyber-physical systems, which combine physical infrastructure with software, sensors, nanotechnology, digital communications technology.

3. The Internet of Things (a multitude of household appliances, appliances or devices connected to the Internet such as refrigerators, washing machines, etc. that will almost constantly report the use of its users) will play a fundamental role.

4. It will allow adding US $ 14.2 trillion to the world economy in the next 10-15 years.

5. It will completely change the world of employment and affect industries across the globe

Klaus Schwab also says in this same book: "The fourth industrial revolution is not defined by a set of emerging technologies in themselves, but by the transition to new systems that are built on the infrastructure of the previous digital revolution."

In this the World Economic Forum wrote about the fourth industrial revolution: "There are three reasons why the current transformations do not represent an extension of the third industrial revolution, but the arrival of a different one: the speed, the scope and the impact in systems. The speed of current advances is unprecedented in history ... And it is interfering with almost every industry in every country. "

Also called 4.0, the revolution follows the other three historical transformative processes: the first marked the transition from manual to mechanized production thanks to innovations such as the steam engine and occurred between 1760 and 1830; the second, around 1850, brought electricity and allowed mass manufacturing.

On the other hand, for the third one, we had to wait until the middle of the 20th century, with the arrival of electronics and information technology and telecommunications.

The fourth turn, millinennials, the Covid-19 crisis and transhumanism

So now in the years 2020-2021 we would be in what the economists and demographers Neil Howe and William Strauss called the stage of the "fourth turn". Howe and Strauss (who died in 2007) made their prediction after developing an original theory that American history unfolds in cycles of approximately 80 years through changes caused by the characteristics of different generations. Among other things, these researchers were the ones who coined the term "millennials" to refer to those born in the early 1980s.

His model also pointed to the arrival of a generational crisis that would force millennials to face a complicated situation at the beginning of their adulthood, in the second decade of this 21st century, which precisely starts with the year 2020.

With the arrival of the Covid-19 crisis, Neil Howe became one of the most questioned voices in outlining possible scenarios after the pandemic, since his theory had managed to predict the current crisis 2020-2021.

Thus in their books "Generations" and in the subsequent "The Fourth Turning" published in 1997, Howe and Strauss asserted that world history is driven by cycles of generations that last between 20 and 23 years. Every four periods, which they called "turns", there is a great crisis. The last great Crisis began with the catastrophic stock market crash known as the "Crack of 1929" and ended after World War II in 1945.

Thus, theoretically, each turn has its own characteristics, but finally, every approximately eighty or ninety years comes the Fourth Turn, a time of political and social crisis "when we reinvent ourselves civically and are reborn as a national community." This period is currently marked by the millennial generation, those born in the 80s.

For the authors, the Fourth Turn began with the financial crisis and the Great Recession of 2008 and will end around 2030. Now, according to Howe, we are in the middle of this phase, which is dangerous.

At this time the Fourth Turn brings with it a trend towards full automation of manufacturing. In fact, the name of the fourth industrial revolution comes from a high-tech strategy project of the German government, on which they have been working since 2013 to bring their production to total independence from human labor.

Automation in this case is carried out by cyber-physical systems, which becomes a reality thanks to the "internet of things" and cloud computing (data storage on internet servers). Thus, cyber-physical systems, which combine physical and tangible machinery with digital processes, are capable of making decentralized decisions and of cooperating with each other and with humans through the internet of things. According to the theorists, it is a "smart factory."

And what about employment?

The basic principle is that companies will be able to create smart networks that can control themselves, throughout the entire value chain, causing shocking economic results as calculated by the consulting firm Accenture in 2015. According to this calculation, an industrial-scale version of this revolution could add US $ 14.2 trillion to the world economy in the next 10-15 years.

At the World Economic Forum in January 2016, they talked about what the most enthusiastic academics had in mind when they talked about Revolution 4.0, that is: nanotechnologies, neurotechnologies, robots, artificial intelligence, biotechnology, energy storage systems, drones and 3D printers, etc.

But unfortunately the fourth revolution could end with five million jobs in the 15 most industrialized countries in the world.

Revolution, for whom?

It is precisely the most advanced countries that will embody the changes more quickly, but at the same time the experts emphasize that it is the emerging economies, which are currently in the Asian continent, which will be able to get the most benefit from it.

The fourth revolution has the potential to raise global income levels and improve the quality of life of entire populations, says Klaus Schwab, the same ones who have benefited from the advent of the digital world (and the possibility of, for example, making payments, listening to music or ordering a taxi from a mobile phone). However, the transformation process will only benefit those who are able to innovate and adapt.

So David Ritter, CEO of Greenpeace Australia / Pacific sums it up in a column about the fourth revolution for the British newspaper The Guardian: "The future of employment will be made of jobs that do not exist, in industries that use new technologies, in planetary conditions that no human being has ever experienced. "

What do businessmen think about the fourth industrial revolution?

According to data from the Global Innovation Barometer for 2016:

70% of executives have positive expectations.

85% believe that innovations in cyber-physical systems will be beneficial.

64% are willing to take the risks of innovating.

17% fear for the negative impact on workers.

In any case, the implementation of the fourth industrial revolution by region is uneven, and it is the emerging markets of Asia, that are mainly adopting the changes in a more disruptive way than their counterparts in developed economies.

According to this same study "Being disruptive (disruptive means that produces a break to promote a radical renewal) is the gold standard for executives and citizens, but it is still a difficult goal to put into practice," the study acknowledges.

Thus, not everyone sees the future with optimism: the polls reflect the concerns of businessmen for "technological Darwinism", where those who do not adapt will not survive.

And if this happens at full speed, as enthusiasts of the fourth revolution point out, the effect may be more devastating than that generated by the third revolution in turn.

The logical consequence is that the revolution will have to write a new relationship between men and robots. But behind there are ethical and social dilemmas to be solved, according to critics and as it seems logical.

Thus, the fear of some critics regarding the fourth industrial revolution is that the elites justify all the changes that this revolution brings as a justification of their values.

Ritter says of the limitations of these changes: "Since maintaining the status quo is not an option, we need a fundamental debate about the shape and objectives of this new economy."

But there are those who do not believe that it is a fourth revolution. Bdale Garbee, a computer specialist who worked for the Debian Project and for Debian GNU / Linux, expresses it with these words: "It is true that the changes are many and very deep, but the concept was first used in 1940 (in a document from a Harvard magazine titled "America's Last Chance," which painted a bleak future due to advancing technology), and its use represents "intellectual laziness."

Other more pragmatic theorists warn that the fourth revolution will only increase inequality in the distribution of income and will bring with it all kinds of geopolitical security dilemmas.

Even the World Economic Forum itself recognizes that "the benefits of the fourth industrial revolution are at risk due to protectionist measures, especially non-tariff and regulatory barriers to world trade, which have been exacerbated since the financial crisis of 2007, which represents a challenge that the fourth revolution will have to face if it wants to deliver what it promises."

Garbee said about the ethical and moral debate on the fourth industrial revolution: "The enthusiasm is not unjustified, these technologies represent amazing advances. But the enthusiasm is no excuse for naivety and history is full of examples of how technology passes through over the social, ethical and political frameworks that we need to make good use of it. "

In fact, transhumanism, which according to Wikipedia is an international cultural and intellectual movement, whose ultimate objective is to transform the human condition through the development and manufacture of widely available technologies that improve human capacities, both at a physical, psychological or intellectual level, It is already opening the debate on what it really means to be human, a debate already opened by gender ideology that recognizes the existence of many sexual genders apart from masculine and feminine, which leads us to ask ourselves what the human being and their sexuality really are . In this way, transhumanism will also open the debate on the type and classes of human beings or transhuman beings that will exist, and that will be the result of implanting parts or devices in their body or brain connected to the internet, whose result is already defended as an evolution of the human being, although perhaps it should be seen rather as an involution. In this way, the old question of how far man can play God may be raised again. It will no longer be about someone who lacks a leg or an arm and putting a prosthesis to improve their quality of life, or someone who has a failing organ to transplant an artificial one printed with 4D technology in him, but to add appendages, pieces or digital devices to the human body or brain to theoretically improve or evolve the human species.

Forecast on the future we are heading to

I would like to be positive about it, but the advance and progress of the globalist agenda since its inception roughly since 1921 with the founding of the Council on Foreign Relations, with the intention of supporting the League of Nations, direct antecedent of the UN, and later With the Bretton Woods agreements and the consequent formation of the World Bank in 1944, and of the United Nations Organization and the International Monetary Fund in 1945, has been continuous and has increasingly spread to more governments of more nations, whose politicians have surrendered to the dogmas and objectives of the globalist agenda with more or less resistance.

In addition, this globalist agenda or New World Order seems to coincide with the situation of the world at the end of time that is described in the bible in the book of Revelation, chapter 17 verses 16 to 18 where a beast will order that no one will buy or sell without that these people first have the sign of the beast "666" placed on their right hand or forehead. Thus says the bible: "He also demanded that everyone — small and large; rich and poor; free and slaves - a mark was placed on their right hand or forehead.17 And no one could buy or sell anything without having that mark, which was either the name of the beast or the number that represents its name. 18 Wisdom is required here. Whoever has understanding, let him solve the meaning of the number of the beast, because it is the number of a man. His number is 666. "

Therefore, it does seem that at the end of time there will be a tight global control over people, which is increasingly possible thanks to new technologies such as 5G internet, which already allows the installation of a multitude of cameras connected to the internet in cities with facial recognition technology for population control, or the internet of things, which allows electronic devices beyond mobile phones, computers or tablets to be connected to the internet and transmit data, such as a refrigerator would send information about each time a certain type of food is missing and automatically place an order online to replace it. Although this technology can be useful in many aspects, it is intrusive and allows us to be controlled and located at all times.

As we well know, new technologies can be useful to us to manage and do many things more quickly and efficiently, but they can also unfortunately serve to better control us.

Although stricter laws are increasingly being legislated regarding the protection of the use of people's private data, and specifically the private data that companies can see or share with other companies, it is well known by lawyers that the laws that are among the ones that are being violated the most today are precisely that of data privacy, starting with technology companies such as Facebook, which in mid-2019 was fined by US regulators with a fine of 5,000 million dollars (about 4,500 million euros), for violating its own policies for the protection of user data, with a data leak of some 87 million users.

This increasingly intense and close control of the population is already taking place today with the restrictions of individual rights and freedoms due to the Covid-19 pandemic, through confinements, curfews, censorship in the social media to unofficial or non-governmental versions about the pandemic, or about unofficial views regarding national or international politics, etc. Even in mid-2021 the implementation of a Covid passport is expected, which will basically consist of a QR code with information about whether we have a negative PCR test, and whether we have all the doses of the Covid-19 vaccine in place to allow ourselves travel or to enter a country. Even later, it is expected for example that they will request this QR code to enter into certain shopping malls, go to concerts, get into the cinema, etc. One of these apps, which will issue the QR code pass called "IATA Travel Pass", is being developed by the IATA airline group in collaboration with the foundation that belongs to the World Economic Forum called "Common Project", while another app with exactly the same purpose will issue the QR code "Common Pass", developed by the Common Project as well.

Even with transhumanism this control by governments or supranational globalist entities can reach a new degree, that is what in theory is the science of improving or taking the human body and mind to a higher level, that is, with the implantation of devices, appendages or chips in the human body or brain that will be connected to the internet and that will transmit data almost continuously to It, which will also be the perfect technology to be able to store all of our private data and to be able to control us better.

Personal vision

I am an evangelical christian and therefore I have a christian worldwiew, that is, I am pro-life and I stand against abortion. So I think that God created man and woman to procreate (worth the redundancy) within marriage, and therefore I do not agree with the LGTBIQ + gender ideology. According to the most classic version of christianity, I believe that it is a sin for a man to have sex with another man or a woman with another woman, or for a person to change sex, because sex is given by God, and this basically can already be observed in a baby's birth according to their genital organs.

But despite my christian worldview, I understand that if other people genuinely think that abortion, euthanasia or LGTBIQ + rights are something correct and that should be defended, I understand that they defend these values, but not impose them on others as if they were the indisputable absolute truth. Thus, for example, it is not really ethical to impose any type of ideology on children at school if their parents do not agree with it, as for example it already happens and even more will happen in Spain with the recently approved educational reform, called Law Celá, approved at the end of December 2020, or for example, I do not think it is ethical to create laws in which if someone by his/her own decision wishes to quit being homosexual, the person who is going to help them with that process is going to be fined.

Ultimately, everyone should live as they want and let others live as they want within the respect of the law, respecting the ideology and ideas of others without imposing them. For example, both the christians must respect people who believe in gender ideology, even if under the protection of freedom of expression they criticize it (the gender ideology) in a respectful way without censorship, such as supporters of gender ideology must respect the faith of Christians.

Conclusion

We advance from about the founding of the Council on Foreign Relations in 1921 towards a globalist agenda imposed on the governments of nations by politicians, financiers, media moguls, directors of pharmaceutical companies and large technological companies, with an agenda contrary to national interests, and this process does not seem to back down.

In addition, as history has shown, the democracies of the nations are in constant danger of extinction by politicians who seek to achieve and perpetuate themselves in power through electoral promises that are often not fulfilled, and with the maintenance of clientelistic networks or benefited classes that receive privileges in order to get their vote and support in return. Furthermore, in many cases these politicians end up changing laws and controlling institutions, undermining the division of powers, and eliminating or censoring the opposition, etc. thus establishing dictatorships to achieve their goal of perpetuating themselves in power.

Thus it is necessary to defend democracies in our nations with well-led demonstrations and civil movements as true patriots, since now the real power struggle is between patriots and globalists, not between politicians of the right and left, who often serve and are controlled for the same globalist agenda.

In fact, we are already experiencing the reduction of our individual rights with the excuse of Covid-19, in what the International Economic Forum calls the largest psychological experiment in the world, to verify how long and where human beings are capable of resisting in the curtailment of our rights and freedoms of movement, expression, religion, etc. Precisely this freedom of expression is also endangered by the censorship imposed by large technology companies and some national governments against those opinions that are different from the official version, regarding major issues such as the Covid-19 pandemic, the result of elections in a nation or the true intentions of politicians or of the people who are part of the globalist entities for example.

Thus, it is necessary to value our individual rights and freedoms and fight for them, demonstrate, protest collectively so that they do not use Covid-19 or any other excuse in order to curtail our rights.

It is also necessary to start migrating to other social media companies that guarantee freedom of expression, which will also open new opportunities to other smaller technological companies.

On the other hand, although better times will surely come at some point, as the bible seems to indicate and as already commented in a previous chapter, in future times there will be an iron control of the population, both of everything that is bought and of what is sold, which is precisely what allows the fourth industrial revolution (control) and its related technologies to do: 5G technology, the internet of things, robotization and intelligent automation of production processes, and also the cybernetic movements associated with these technologies such as transhumanism.

The globalist agenda as explained is just as dangerous and harmful for christians, muslims, people of any religion, philosophy, agnostics and atheists, because its objective is that sovereign nations lose more and more power and autonomy in favor of a globalist elite not elected by the people, who imposes their agenda in an authoritarian way and each time also in a more open way.

Ultimately, these elites are not interested in defending the rights of groups excluded from society, immigrants, the LGTBIQ + collective, etc., but rather in taking advantage of the defense of these rights to subvert the internal order, eroding national values, and thus being able to create a society more susceptible to the globalist agenda and have an excuse for the implantation of this dictatorship.

So for our sake when it comes to voting for our rulers, let us bear in mind that there are still politicians, almost always from the political right, who, although unpopular for many people, still oppose the imposition of the globalist agenda through their different dogmas.

Thus, we can agree or not with the gender ideology, with abortion, euthanasia, etc., but regardless of our beliefs about these ideologies, we must know that they are used for the imposition of a world dictatorship, because globalist elites are at heart interested in controlling the world following their own agenda, and not much in defending the rights of the people. If they were really interested in defending the rights and freedoms of the people, they would not try to impose a world globalist agenda, knowing that no one has voted or legitimized them to do so.

For questions or comments about this book, you can write to me at: cesar.munoz.madrigal@gmail.com

Bibliography and sources consulted

- César Vidal's book "A changing world" published in 2019, has been the general reference work to document me about the dogmas of the globalist agenda, the icons of the globalist agenda and the resistance to the globalist agenda.

-The YouTube video of the Financial Times mentioned in the chapter on "Personal Testimony" can be found in English with the title "Why capitalism needs to be reset in 2020", published on December 30st, 2019, in the following link: https://youtu.be/3MKvVcQuD4E

- Regarding the geologist expert in climate change Don Easterbrook and his session in the United States Senate dated March 26, 2013, which I mentioned in the chapter on "Personal Testimony", the original video in English can be found on YouTube at this link: https://youtu.be/udTS_O1f7-E, with the title "Senate Hearing on climate change".

- Regarding the astrophysicist and climate scientist, Dr. Willie Soon, who I mentioned in the chapter "Personal Testimony", regarding to the effect of the sun on global warming and regarding sunspots, the video on YouTube with this conference can be found under the title: "The sun also warms: Dr. Willie Son Shows the sun-Climate Connection" on the following link: https://youtu.be/KazGXAqqkds

-The YouTube video titled "The in-depth story behind a climate fraud" investigated and narrated by Dr. John Robson, who is the executive director of the Climate Discussion Nexus, and who made me understand why there is no global scientific consensus on the 97% on global warming, can be found in English at the following link: https://youtu.be/ewJ6Tl8ccAw

- The data on the "Fourth Industrial Revolution" that appear in the chapter with this very same title, have been mainly taken from the article by Valeria Perasso published in the newspaper ABC Mundo under the title "What is the fourth industrial revolution and why should we care?), which can be found at the following link: https://www.bbc.com/mundo/noticias-37631834

- The information about the Fourth Turn was partially extracted from an article published on June 25, 2020, in the newspaper "Infobae" under the title "The fourth turn:

the grim warning of Neil Howe, the historian who predicted a serious crisis in 2020" , which can be found in Spanish at the following link:

https://www.infobae.com/america/mundo/2020/06/25/el-cuarto-giro-la-sombria-advertencia-de-neil-howe-el-historiador-que-predijo-una-grave- crisis-in-2020 /

Thanks to all of them for contributing to the documentation of this book.

Manufactured by Amazon.ca
Bolton, ON